'If you want to take a fresh look at the Bible and its relevance for today, then this is the book for you. Providing readers with a fascinating panoramic view of the Bible, *Life after Life* examines several important apologetic themes and so-called difficult biblical texts. It focuses on the resurrection and shows how the Bible is designed to lead its readers from reflecting on the reality of death to considering life in all its fullness and rich meaning. It also highlights the significance of the longing for eternal life in each of our hearts.'

Sergiy Tymchenko, President, REALIS Christian Center, Kyiv, Ukraine

T0326750

LIFE AFTER LIFE

Mark Meynell is Director (Europe and Caribbean) of Langham Preaching. He has been in ordained ministry for more than twenty-five years. He was on the senior team at All Souls Church, Langham Place, London, for nine years, during which he served as a part-time chaplain in HM Treasury, HMRC and the Cabinet Office. Prior to that, he taught at a small seminary in Kampala, Uganda, for four years. Since 2019, he has helped to bring the Hutchmoot Arts conference to the UK and in 2022 completed a Doctor of Ministry (at Covenant Theological Seminary, St Louis) researching the place of the arts in cultural apologetics. Mark and his wife, Rachel, have two grown-up children, and they live in Maidenhead, Berkshire.

LIFE AFTER LIFE

Why Jesus means death isn't the end

Mark Meynell

INTER-VARSITY PRESS
SPCK Group, Studio 101, The Record Hall, 16–16A Baldwin's Gardens,
London EC1N 7RJ, England
Email: ivp@ivpbooks.com
Website: www.ivpbooks.com

First published 2024

British Library Cataloguing-in-Publication Data
A catalogue record for this book is available from the British Library.

ISBN: 978–1–78974–500–9
eBook ISBN: 978–1–78974–501–6

Set in 11/14 Minion Pro
Typeset in Great Britain by Fakenham Prepress Solutions, Fakenham, Norfolk
Printed in Great Britain by Clays Limited
Produced on paper from sustainable sources

Inter-Varsity Press publishes Christian books that are true to the Bible
and that communicate the gospel, develop discipleship and strengthen the church for
its mission in the world.

IVP originated within the Inter-Varsity Fellowship, now the Universities and Colleges
Christian Fellowship, a student movement connecting Christian Unions in
universities and colleges throughout Great Britain, and a member movement of the
International Fellowship of Evangelical Students. Website: www.uccf.org.uk. That
historic association is maintained, and all senior IVP staff and committee members
subscribe to the UCCF Basis of Faith.

To the Langham Preaching Global Leadership Team –
colleagues, friends, inspirations each one –
Femi Adeleye, Esteban and Igor Amestegui, Jennifer Cuthbertson,
Dwi Maria Handayani, Ruth Slater and Paul Windsor.

Contents

Foreword

I'm a pastor's son from a small town in the American South. If you're familiar with American culture, you can deduce quite a bit about me from that one sentence. You might surmise that I grew up in a racially troubled culture, or that I had a bit of a drawl, or that I have a love for colourful storytelling, and you would be correct. You might also correctly assume that I grew up going to church and going to church *a lot*. Ours was a generally healthy church situation, and I have no real complaints about the structure and community it provided for me and the rest of our little town. I enjoyed seeing my friends at Sunday night youth group; church camp was great because they had a swimming pool; the weekly Bible study was fine even though it prevented me from ever watching a single episode of *The Greatest American Hero*, a Wednesday night show my less-spiritual high school friends loved. Church culture also provided scrumptious and recurring potluck dinners, which are the best way to experience southern American cuisine – or any cuisine, for that matter. As for more theological matters, like pretty much everyone else in our town, I believed in God. I didn't have a hard time believing in Jesus *as* God. It all made a kind of sense to me as a budding musician who caught strains of the music of the spheres when I sat alone by the lake at night, and as a budding writer and poet who found himself strangely moved by old hymns and older psalms. I don't mean to paint too rosy a picture of my childhood. There was plenty of awfulness, too. But the point is, Church was the water I swam in. Nearly every corner of our lives was touched by it, not least because the parsonage was right next to the church. I could see the steeple from my bedroom window.

And yet, even with all that exposure to Christian culture (if not always Christianity), I somehow missed something central to the whole thing. See, we talked a lot about heaven, but not so much about the new creation. We talked a lot about an afterlife, but not so much about resurrection. We talked a lot about Jesus conquering sin, but not so much about his victory over death. To be fair, it's possible our church did talk about those things and I just wasn't paying attention. But many years later, after reading some good theology that cast a biblical vision of where the whole story of the cosmos is heading, I was stunned that I had missed it.

I also realised that my high school years, during which I hardly claimed any association with Jesus, were plagued with a sense of futility. Why futility? Because, even if I assented to a belief in God, and in Christ *as* God, and even if I could accept the fact of his love for me, deep down a bigger question lurked: *so what?* What was it all *for?* We were all given these bodies to live in, in what I considered a breathtakingly beautiful world – a world jammed with story and poetry and art and music, a world overflowing with sunsets and crescent moons and glimmering stars and lush valleys – and as I understood it at the time our bodies were bad and the whole earth was going to burn because it was bad, too. It didn't do any good to think too much about heaven because it was utterly different from this world. It was 'spiritual' – which I took to mean 'non-material' – and whatever was waiting for us on the other side of the veil would surely involve singing forever and ever in some mysterious, disembodied form. The poems and epic tales and lovely songs didn't really matter because they belonged to *this* world; the mountains didn't matter, nor did rivers or great herons or maple leaves in autumn. I realise now that I was busy trying to soak up all the goodness this world had to offer because I suspected I might not like the next world very much, no matter how much I was told I ought to.

I'm no church historian, but I suppose there was an insidious strain of Gnosticism that had snuck into our part of the American church, insinuating, if not outright declaring, that all matter is bad or is at least to be viewed with suspicion. Meanwhile I felt secretly guilty for loving this world so much – the wide and abundant skies of Florida as well as the wide and abundant tables of food at those church potluck dinners. Heaven, I was told, is going to be better than this accursed place: better without bodies, without food, without a planet, better because it's going to be like an eternal church service. (Trust me, if you want to pique a longing for Jesus in a child, don't tell them that.) Try as I might, I could not muster much excitement about life after death.

My dad officiated at most of the funerals in our town, so by the time I left home I had seen quite a few corpses in our church building. Many of those dead bodies belonged to people I knew, and in that context death didn't freak me out. I wasn't afraid of it – but even as a Christian, I wasn't thrilled about what lay on the other side. I lived more like a convicted criminal who had a few weeks of freedom before his sentence began. It's a long story, but I soon came to truly believe that Jesus is God and he loves me, which meant that the notion of being with him forever trumped any mis-givings I might have had about what exactly we'll all be doing up there for eternity. He is enough, and I trust him. But then the good news got even better.

At some point I realised, with a rush of wonder, that God loves mountains and rivers and great herons, too. It's right there in Genesis. He loves potluck dinners. It's right there in Jesus' parables, not to mention his feeding of the multitudes. Matter, it turns out, matters. The resurrected Christ liked to eat (Luke 24:30, 41). He liked to cook, too (John 21:9). And Paul tells us that we'll have bodies like his (Philippians 3:21). I wish someone had told me when I was young that God in fact loves this place. I wish someone had told me that in John 3:16 the word translated 'world' is the Greek word *kosmos*: for God so loved the *cosmos* that he gave his only begotten Son (John 3:16). When I realised that this very planet, the one where I'm sitting as I write this, is the same one God called very good; when I realised that Revelation tells us about a new Jerusalem coming down out of heaven; when I real-ised that resurrection means I'll have a body like Jesus does, and that body will work and laugh and feast under the gaze of a good King – well, I had my answer to the question that haunted me as a young man.

Foreword

This, friends, is what it's all for. Glorious and undying bodies. The marriage of heaven and earth. A new creation made more beautiful by the redemption of the original. A river and a tree and a great city. A world to care for and reign over. A world where we dwell with God, and he with us. I don't think it's a stretch to expect that we'll have stories and poems and songs to write, gardens to tend, mountains to climb, cities to wander through, meals to cook. To love this world is to practise loving the next. I don't merely long to worship Jesus; I long to eat with him.

Mark has written exactly the kind of book I wish I had read as a young man brimming with questions about death and especially about what comes after. I've had many conversations with Mark and am always surprised by how wide his interests range and how deep his knowledge goes. Here he's brought that breadth and depth to a truly universal subject, refusing to shy away from the spectre of death and reminding us that it has truly been defeated by Christ. May this book unfold a little more of the glory of the good news to you.

Andrew Peterson
Singer/songwriter and writer, Nashville

Acknowledgements

I recently read an article by the British philosopher Julian Baggini in which he suggests that publishers should take a leaf out of the film industry. Even though most viewers start leaving their seats or flipping channels the moment the credits roll, no production company would dream of omitting any of the contributors. No film would ever reach a screen without the likes of third Gaffer or second Clapper-loader, of Foley Artists, Focus Pullers or Dolly Grips. It matters little that a person's task is menial or invisible. Each is a valued member of the team. So Baggini thinks that books should do something similar, listing every contributor or support (however brief or seemingly unrelated their help was), even if the credits take up several pages at the end. He does have a point.

Writing a book, despite all the hours that a writer spends in isolation, is never an individual business (however much he or she might like to burnish the image of the *auteur* pouring out inspired brilliance from a secluded hermitage). So, by rights, I should name all the staff of the many coffee shops and libraries where I worked on this. Sadly, I read Baggini's article too late for that. Pride of place should obviously go to the family – to Rachel first and foremost for her support and encouragement; and also to Josh and Zanna for enduring dad jokes (actually quite funny) and niche references (actually quite interesting). Although the fact that they've both left home now might tell you something. I must also thank the wonderful Fraser family (David and Gail, Esther-Gail and Cara, Daniel and Kara). Old friends from their time in London, they endured me in their Kingston home for a whole week when I found myself unexpectedly stuck in Jamaica (nice problem to have). I was able to get some good work done. Various friends read parts or all of the book as it emerged, and all offered helpful comments and encouragements: Sam Allberry, David Goode, Slavko Hadzic, Julian Hardyman, Becca Reynolds and Sergiy Tymchenko. I'm especially grateful to Ed Moll, who went above and beyond, applying his eagle-eye to a close reading of the whole manuscript in detail. Huge thanks to Andrew for writing his generous and poignant foreword. Here's to the next longish walk in roughly the same direction, AP!

A big thank you to the Keswick Convention for the honour of an invitation to write this book, especially Elizabeth McQuoid, James Robson and James's successor, Mark Ellis. It has been good to be back with IVP for this one and I've enjoyed getting to know and work with Josh Wells and other members of the team. It's lovely to reconnect with Mary Davis too!

Finally, this book is dedicated to the team I'm honoured to have been a part of for a decade: Langham Preaching's Global Leadership Team. Perhaps the most precious gift of being involved in this work (in various roles since 2002) has been the deep friendships that grow very naturally as a result. It is a rare privilege indeed to have dear friends in almost every corner of the globe. This is a small token of my gratitude and appreciation: Femi Adeleye (Africa Director) in Accra, Ghana; Igor Amestegui (Latin America Director), his son Esteban (Igor's PA and Media Assistant), both in Cochabamba, Bolivia; Jennifer Cuthbertson (Coordinator for Facilitator Development) on Vancouver Island, Canada; Dwi Maria Handayani (Asia and South Pacific Director) in Bandung, Indonesia; Ruth Slater (Associate Programme Director) in Carlisle, UK; and Paul Windsor (Programme Director) in Auckland, New Zealand.

Maidenhead, Berkshire

S. D. G.

Introduction

Throughout the British Isles and northern France, you will often find an ancient yew tree dominating a cemetery or churchyard. These trees are truly remarkable, growing to a height of between ten and twenty metres, and, occasionally, as high as twenty-eight metres. They are hard to date, however, because trunks and branches often hollow out, only for new offshoots to regenerate from apparently lifeless stumps. So, while many are between four and six hundred years old, some could well have been living for two millennia. For example, the Fortingall Yew, in a Perthshire village in Scotland, is thought to predate the Roman occupation of Britain and may even be five millennia in age, making it one of the oldest trees in Europe. In the village of La Haye-de-Routot in north-west France, the churchyard contains two yew trees each of at least a thousand years in age. The hollow trunk of one of them was so wide that it is said to have contained forty standing adults without too much of a squash.

Why the association with cemeteries? The simplest answer, for England at least, is that King Edward I ordered yews to be planted near churches. But there must be more to it. It seems that the connection between the yew tree and death predates Christianity. For one thing, the entire tree is toxic so ingesting even a relatively small quantity of yew berries or leaves is dangerous. There is still no known antidote (although medication mitigates symptoms). So perhaps the yew's significance was no more complex than that. They were planted in places of death as bringers of death. Or simpler still, these trees were placed deliberately to discourage farmers from allowing livestock to wander onto sacred, communal spaces.

But it seems that yews had an even deeper significance. One crucial aspect is that they are evergreens. This means that, like the

Norway Spruce (the most common species used for Christmas trees), it keeps its leaves in winter, as the word implies. In the long, dispiriting bitterness of a northern European winter, plants that retained their greenery felt reassuring. They kept dwindling hopes of spring alive, even in the darkest days of late December and early January. It is not hard to see why this might resonate in a cemetery for those who believe that death is not the end. They were symbols of hope. Factor in their extraordinary longevity and apparent ability to regenerate even after age and disease have hollowed out their trunks as well, and they are ripe for Christian symbolism especially. Yew trees represent death, new birth to new life, and eternity *simultaneously*.

Death is the universal human experience, the ultimate statistic, the last great enemy. But it is impossible to contemplate death without also considering life. They are inseparable. The significance of a person's life is always called into question by death. At the same time, death nearly always provokes a longing, the yearning for something afterwards. The vast majority of belief systems around the world have imagined some form of afterlife. So, it is unsurprising that even in the secular West, most are reluctant to abandon the aspiration altogether. They might have embraced the materialism of the New Atheists, such that this world is all that exists, with eternity, gods and souls dismissed as mere superstition. Yet when a loved one dies, they still cling to comforting platitudes like 'she's in a better place', 'we'll meet again' or even 'he lives on in our memories'. Hope for the beyond is deeply ingrained.

This is a book about that hope. It is not a book about wishful thinking. Nor is it simply about gazing into the mists of an eternal but remote future. This is hope that is earthy and rooted, hope as much about the here and now as it is about a certain future. This is because this hope is first and foremost about *life*. In many ways, this book is a companion to *Cross-Examined*, and there is some inevitable, though limited, overlap.[1] If the earlier book's centre of gravity was the atonement, this book focuses on Christ's

---

1 Mark Meynell, *Cross-Examined*, revised and expanded ed. (London: IVP, 2021).

resurrection as a foundation for exploring matters of life and death from various corners of Scripture:

Part 1 explores the Old Testament's groundwork for New Testament hope of life after death. Life is God's idea, after all. He made it and he sustains it. But are there any hints at plans for dealing with the problem of our mortality? We will discover several different threads but see that these will only be brought together by Jesus himself.

Part 2 looks at how Jesus fulfils those new life expectations, both for himself and for those who put their trust in him.

Part 3 considers what life after this life might actually be like. For that we must turn to the Apostle John's vision in the book of Revelation. This is the heart of Christian hope.

The Appendix offers a brief summary of the historical evidence for Christ's resurrection.

Life is God's idea. He created it. He sustains it. He loves it and generously gives it, even *after* death.

> And if the Spirit of him who raised Jesus from the dead is living in you, he who raised Christ from the dead will also give life to your mortal bodies because of his Spirit who lives in you.
> (Romans 8:11)

Questions to consider

1 What do friends and neighbours understand by 'hope'? How does this differ from or resonate with Christian hope?
2 How much do you think about what happens after death? Do you feel hopeful, fearful or something else?

3

Part 1

PAST: LIFE FOR THE DEAD

If God created life itself, then why does death come about in the first place? With consequences so devastating for human significance and suffering, does it always have the last word?

God might have had every reason to abandon what he had made after the Fall, but he refuses to. He perseveres and throughout the Old Testament, we see that the groundwork is laid for New Testament expectations of life after death. This is hinted at in various ways in the course of the Bible's grand story. God is concerned to protect and save life, which is why he both forbids human sacrifice and provides alternative sacrifices (as with Abraham and Isaac, for example). As we will see, this concern presents him with dilemmas that only he can resolve, dilemmas that converge on God's purpose for the kings on David's throne. Even though the Old Testament writers do not yet have all the answers for how he can do that, they clearly look forward to the time when God's King will bring his people through death and into new life after this life.

1

Life and death: the breath, blood and barrier

Origins: breath of life (Genesis 2)

and breathed into his nostrils the breath of life (Genesis 2:7)

Mary Shelley was only twenty when *Frankenstein* was first published in 1818. She could never have predicted the book's astonishing longevity. It is now embedded in Western culture. Two centuries on, Victor Frankenstein and his monster have become shorthand for scientific progress and invention returning to haunt its creators. Shelley's subtitle was telling: *The Modern Prometheus*. She was inspired by one version of the Greek myth about Prometheus, a god commissioned to make human beings and prepare them ready for Zeus, king of the gods, to animate them with life. When Zeus punished human beings for the poor quality of their offerings to him, he refused them the gift of fire. Prometheus stole it for them – for which his gruesome punishment was an eternity chained to a rock from which an eagle would peck out his constantly regenerating liver! Shelley's implication is clear: young Frankenstein was essentially attempting to replicate a combination of Prometheus' and Zeus' creative act… with devastating, unintended consequences.

If you have seen one of its countless cinema adaptations, you will assume that Shelley's book relishes arcane and intimidating features in Victor's laboratory. After all, most film-sets show chemical flasks bubbling with noxious-looking potions heated by antiquated contraptions designed to harness the power of lightning bolts. It is archetypal steampunk! This is hardly surprising, because it is the crux of the entire novel: a human being artificially given life by a fellow human. Yet, Shelley barely describes the moment at all. She was not, after all, intentionally forging the genre of science fiction, and she was not especially interested in the science of it. The only thing we learn from Victor's account of that dreary November night is this: 'I collected the instruments of life around me, that I might infuse a spark of being into the lifeless thing that lay at my feet.'[1] Then, in the same paragraph, but without even a hint of how this 'infusion' would take place, it has suddenly already happened. At one o'clock in the morning, 'by the glimmer of the half-extinguished light, I saw the dull yellow eye of the creature opened; it breathed hard, and a convulsive motion agitated its limbs. How can I describe my emotions at this catastrophe?'[2] Of course, Frankenstein the scientist has little sense of quite how catastrophic this moment will be, but the narrative is full of foreboding.

Naturally, there have been hundreds of interpretations of its significance since. One critic put it bluntly by commenting that, 'Frankenstein is a book about what happens when a man tries to have a baby without a woman,' which is certainly true![3] But what strikes me every time about this is something even more basic. Nobody knows Victor's secret. Nobody knows the secret of life. Not even the greatest scientific minds have even begun to figure it out. We understand DNA, we have mapped the human genome, we can do wonders with stem cells and test tubes. Biochemical marvels seem to hit the headlines on a monthly basis. And yet... the existence of life is still essentially a mind-boggling mystery. This doesn't stop billionaires from having their corpses cryogenically frozen on the off chance that the secret of life gets discovered. I can think of better uses for their funds, quite frankly. For the truth is, we know a million ways of ending a life, but for all our biochemical sophistication and knowledge, only God knows how to start one.

---

1   Mary Shelley, *Frankenstein: Or, the modern Prometheus* (London: Penguin Classics, 2003), p. 58.
2   Shelley, *Frankenstein*, p. 58.
3   Anne K. Mellor, *Mary Shelley: Her life, her fiction, her monsters* (London: Routledge, 1988), p. 40.

So, there is a sense of stepping onto holy ground when we open Genesis 1–2. Like Mary Shelley's antihero, God does not reveal his secret for life – but there the similarities end. There is nothing diabolical or catastrophic in the creation of man and woman. We find little drama, no blind experimental alleys, a complete absence of fanfare. It is simply one more stage, albeit a climactic one, in the kaleidoscopic vision of God's creation.

> Then the LORD God formed a man from the dust of the ground and *breathed into his nostrils the breath of life*, and the man became a living being.
> (Genesis 2:7, my emphasis)

One moment we are told there is a beautiful, inert body, crafted in divinely appointed physical perfection; the next minute his heart beats, blood pumps, lungs inflate and synapses fire. All at once. As if it is the result of divine CPR (cardiopulmonary resuscitation). Although, to be strictly accurate, this is no resuscitation. It is an unprecedented, revolutionary animation. In one instant, the creature goes from lifeless sculpture to 'life-filled' person. Of course, Genesis is no scientific analysis but a work of theology, although it is no less authoritative or significant for that. The crucial thing to notice is that life is both God's idea and God's gift. Without this astonishing, divine act, there is no way for 'the man [to become] a living being.' This means that, as Genesis tells it, there is an organic, even biological, connection between human life and our Creator. Without him, there is no life.

This helps to explain the sheer wonder of life, doesn't it? On the one hand, it is the most normal thing in the world. None of us knows anything of *not* being alive. And yet, when we stop to reflect for a moment, the fact that we are conscious and breathing is… well, breath-taking. To be alive and also to know we are alive. Many blithely stumble through the months and years without reflecting on the weirdness of that. Not for too long, that is. It raises too many knotty problems, the big Why? Where from? Who? What? questions.

Some insist we are mere biological accidents, unplanned consequences of random chemical reactions stretching back into deep time, and thus in the cosmic scheme of things, we are largely if not entirely irrelevant. As scientist Stephen Jay Gould put it,

> Humans arose, rather, as a fortuitous and contingent outcome of thousands of linked events, any one of which could have occurred differently and sent history on an alternate pathway that would not have led to consciousness.[4]

The outlook from this perspective is bleak. There is no purpose or design; no narrative to belong to; no explanation to draw comfort from. There are few better articulations of such a view than that of Shakespeare's power-lusting Scottish king, Macbeth, moments after learning of his wife's suicide. His enemies have assembled their forces outside his castle and so he knows what the following day holds (although at this point, he is still confident of victory).

> Tomorrow, and tomorrow, and tomorrow
> Creeps in this petty pace from day to day,
> To the last syllable of recorded time,
> And all our yesterdays have lighted fools
> The way to dusty death. Out, out, brief candle!
> Life's but a walking shadow, a poor player
> That struts and frets his hour upon the stage
> And then is heard no more. It is a tale
> Told by an idiot. Full of sound and fury,
> Signifying nothing.
> (*Macbeth*, Act 5, Scene 5)

Who is the 'idiot' in this telling? Those who think there is anything special about being human, those who imagine it is worth

---

4   Stephen Jay Gould in C. C. Gaither and A. E. Cavazos-Gaither, *Gaither's Dictionary of Scientific Quotations*, vols 1 and 2 (New York, NY: Springer, 2008), p. 223.

even trying to craft a story about a life. For whenever they do, it can only be 'full of sound and fury, signifying nothing'. Which is why it is poignant indeed to find that one of the greatest American storytellers of the last century, Ernest Hemingway, commented, 'Life is just a dirty trick – a short journey from nothingness to nothingness.' After that it comes as no surprise that he would take his own life in 1961, just as his father had done, and, in time, as his brother Leicester and sister Ursula would do.[5]

And yet... and yet... This simply does not feel right. That is hardly a conclusive argument in itself, of course. But it is hard to deny the sense most of us have that life is a precious gift, that it matters, even when logic might insist otherwise. The doctrine of a Creator God certainly buttresses such a belief, something even Jean-Paul Sartre, the French existentialist philosopher, conceded weeks before his death. He wrote to his friend Pierre Victor:

> I do not feel that I am a product of chance, a speck of dust in the universe, but someone who was expected, prepared, pre-figured. In short, a being whom only a Creator could put here; and this idea of a creating hand refers to God.[6]

This did not make him a believer. On another occasion, he famously lamented, 'that God does not exist, I cannot deny. That my whole being cries out for God, I cannot forget.'[7] So perhaps our yearning for significance really is mere egotistical wishful thinking. But if so, why do so many of us share this yearning? A coincidence? Couldn't it just be possible that we yearn for the very thing we were created to yearn for? C. S. Lewis famously made this point a linchpin of his ground-breaking *Mere Christianity*.

---

5   Tragically, it seems the Hemingway family shared a hereditary propensity to iron build-up in the body, which causes physical and mental deterioration.

6   Norman L. Geisler, *Is Man the Measure? Contemporary humanism* (Grand Rapids, MI: Baker, 1983), p. 46.

7   Jean-Paul Sartre, *Essays in Aesthetics*, ed. Wade Baskin (New York, NY: Philosophical Library, 2014), p. 10.

The Christian says, 'Creatures are not born with desires unless satisfaction for those desires exists. A baby feels hunger: well, there is such a thing as food. A duckling wants to swim: well, there is such a thing as water. Men feel sexual desire: well, there is such a thing as sex. If I find in myself a desire which no experience in this world can satisfy, the most probable explanation is that I was made for another world. If none of my earthly pleasures satisfy it, that does not prove that the universe is a fraud. Probably earthly pleasures were never meant to satisfy it, but only to arouse it, to suggest the real thing.'[8]

There is something inherently good and beautiful about life, and I'm not just talking about human life. Despite the myriad oddities and perplexities of the natural world, all life and lives are remarkable. So, when out walking our dog in the mornings, I occasionally find myself stopped in my tracks by the thought that this peculiar but lovable, non-human lifeform recognises my voice and face, that she seems excited to see me if I've been out for the day, and how she expresses delight at the simplest of pleasures. What's more, she has been a real comfort and encouragement to each of us in the family at some of our darker moments. How mysterious!

As for human life, that is truly astonishing. It sometimes leaves us speechless. I will never forget holding each of our children within seconds of their births, profoundly aware that my life was irrevocably changed by these tiny, brand new, precious lives. Now that they are in their twenties, it's hard to believe how much they have changed and grown since those first seconds. Yet they are recognisably the same people! Is it any wonder that even the staunchest sceptics struggle to avoid words like 'miracle' in the hospital delivery room? Furthermore, while there are many characteristics that humans share with the animal kingdom, and indeed all living things, there are many things that seem to set us apart. The relationship I have with our dog doesn't even compare with

---

8   C. S. Lewis, *Mere Christianity*, 26th ed. (London: Collins, 1990), pp. 118–19.

my love for the children; they are on completely different planes. There are aspects of being human that set us apart. The focal point for our distinctiveness is that weighty mystery of being created 'in the image of God' (Genesis 1:27).[9]

Then, if we consider the other end of the journey, we are confronted by a parallel mystery. Why is it that there is a universal sense of loss when a person dies? If death is merely the fact of life that we all know it to be – or as *The Lion King* would have it, simply part of the 'circle of life' – why do we recoil so much? The renowned psychiatrist, Elisabeth Kübler-Ross, spent many years observing how her terminally ill patients came to terms with their mortality. She published her influential book *On Death and Dying* in 1969, in which she explained her observation of five distinct stages through which people progressed (although she insisted that there was no set order):[10]

- *denial* (a resistance to the prognosis or clinging to alternative explanations)
- *anger* (at the sense of the unfairness of it all, or perhaps expressed in acute frustration with loved ones)
- *bargaining* (depending on their beliefs, patients might bargain with God for extra time to last until a family event, or pledge a lifestyle change)
- *depression* (a feeling of hopelessness at our mortality, becoming withdrawn or antisocial)
- *acceptance* (a calm embrace of reality, which can be unsettling for surviving loved ones).

Kübler-Ross's observations were speedily adopted as equally helpful for grieving survivors, although there have been numerous tweaks and adaptations to the model. But many still ignore the bigger question. Why are there any stages of grief at all? Sure,

---

9 Sadly, this is not the place for going into detail. One brief place to follow up is Mark Meynell, *What Makes Us Human*, Questions Christians Ask (London: Good Book Company, 2015).

10 Elisabeth Kübler-Ross, *On Death and Dying: What the dying have to teach* (London: Routledge, 2009).

we always need to adapt and adjust to new circumstances, especially when they are as disorienting as losing a family member. But human beings are very good at adapting. Why do we still mourn, sometimes for months, sometimes for years? Could it not be because there *is* something profoundly difficult, or even alien, about death? All death, even the passing of a chronically ill loved one for whom death might be seen as bringing relief. The Apostle Paul wrote 'the last enemy to be destroyed is death' (1 Corinthians 15:26). He clearly means by this that death is something that beats us. It always has the last word as the great, universal leveller. Nobody has ever beaten death at its own game. We will return to this in due course. But is Paul not also implying that death is our enemy because it is fundamentally wrong? It is far from the ideal that God wanted for us. That is surely why we hate it so much. But then, this makes perfect sense if life is inherently a beautiful gift from our Creator. He breathed life into the first man, initiating an incredible biological chain reaction that has continued for millennia. Life is a divinely created miracle. This changes everything.

Martin Luther King Jr grounded his life's work, and indeed the entire struggle for civil rights, on this truth. He drew on it with unerring frequency, whether on momentous occasions such as his Lincoln Memorial speech at the 1963 March on Washington and his Nobel Peace Prize acceptance speech in 1964, or in negotiations and debates. Our createdness was the strongest, and perhaps only sure, basis on which to defend the dignity and value of human beings regardless of their race. If our lives are indeed the result of God breathing 'the breath of life' into Adam's nostrils – then not only is the fact of existence precious, but so is each individual human life. Thus, as historian Tom Holland brilliantly explained,

The evolution of the concept of human rights... derived, not from ancient Greece or Rome, but from the period of history condemned by all right-thinking revolutionaries as a lost millennium, in which any hint of enlightenment had at once been snuffed out by monkish book-burning fanatics. It was an inheritance from the lawyers of the Middle Ages.[11]

And where did those lawyers from the Middle Ages derive their ideas about human rights? The Scriptures, and in particular their common conviction that human beings are all being created in God's image.

This is the foundational truth on which this entire book is based. God created life and it is an inspiring thing. We are fearfully and wonderfully made. But we cannot stop there.

Catastrophe: barred from life (Genesis 3)[12]

a sword... to guard the tree of life (Genesis 3:24)

If life is so great, then, the obvious question is 'why must it end?' Why does God allow for human mortality at all? The shock from Genesis 3 is that divine permission is not the issue. Human mortality is the result of a divine sanction.

As the Genesis creation accounts tell it, water is clearly fundamental to life. It exists in the chaos, but God's creative ordering means separating out the various environments, such that some will inhabit the water, others the land and air. But all will depend on water. This is evident by the often-missed detail in God's preparation of the earth for biological life.

> Now no shrub had yet appeared on the earth and no plant had yet sprung up, for the LORD God had not sent rain on the earth and there was no one to work the ground, but streams came up from the earth and watered the whole surface of the ground.
> (Genesis 2:5–6)

---

11 Tom Holland, *Dominion* (London: Little, Brown, 2019), p. 386.

12 A fuller exposition of Genesis 3 is given in Mark Meynell, *Cross-Examined*, revised and expanded ed. (London: IVP, 2021), chapters 3–4.

We might wish it otherwise, but our fragile lives are as dependent today on this primordial provision as they ever were. As one anonymous wit put it, 'Man, despite his artistic pretensions, his sophistication and many accomplishments, owes the fact of his existence to a six-inch layer of topsoil and the fact that it rains.' This makes environmental devastation all the more insane, as Chris Wright recently pointed out.

> I find it hard to think of a clearer example of the sheer lunacy of human folly than for the same people at almost the same time to be searching for fresh water on the moon (where we might never live), while intentionally destroying vast quantities of the diminishing store of the precious stuff on the earth (where we actually do live).[13]

We see this dependence in the description of that special quarter designated for the man and woman, the Garden of Eden. We are told of four rivers that feed it, which gives the reader a sense of geographical specificity: the Pishon flowing around Havilah, Gihon around Cush, Tigris east of Assyria, and the Euphrates (Genesis 2:11–14). All is not as it seems, however. There is something deliberately inconceivable in the way it gets mapped out. Two of these rivers are well known even today. The Tigris and Euphrates flow through what is now Iraq, sustaining life in the great cities of Babylon and Nineveh in the ancient world and Baghdad and Mosul today; the territory bounded by these river systems is known as Mesopotamia (literally, meaning 'between rivers' in Greek). However, Pishon and Gihon are mythological. Ever since it was written, all kinds of suggestions have been offered: the Roman–Jewish historian Josephus speculated that Pishon was the Ganges in India; mediaeval rabbis wondered if it was the Nile in Egypt. But it is unlikely we were ever meant to know. The simple point is that life in paradise is inconceivable without water.

---

13 Christopher J. H. Wright, 'Looking for Water on the Moon – Destroying It on the Earth', *Transform (Langham Partnership News)*, autumn 2023, https://uk.langham.org/news-and-updates/transform-autumn-2023/, (accessed 18 January 2024).

Another result of Eden's mythic geography is that its scale is impossible to imagine. It is a vast area so to get a sense of this, it is probably necessary to think in terms of countries rather than country estates. That immediately throws God's provision in an entirely new light. All too often, people perceive God to be restrictive and a killjoy, which is why he keeps on making rules such as his terms and conditions for living in Eden. But if the garden is the size of a country, his instructions are anything but restrictive, aren't they? He says, 'You are free to eat from any tree in the garden' (Genesis 2:16). Consider that for a moment. Think of all the trees that exist in your country. Imagine that you have access to the fruit from literally all of them. To be warned of just one tree out of perhaps millions is not exactly hard. The key decision, I suppose, boils down to your environment preference. If Eden is like the UK, then, you can choose between rolling hills, craggy coastline, atmospheric moorland, dense forests and idyllic lakes. It is all included. That is overwhelming freedom! Only now can we begin to grasp the context of God's restriction: 'but you must not eat from the tree of the knowledge of good and evil, for when you eat from it you will certainly die' (Genesis 2:17).

So, it is a choice between millions and one. Of course, it is not quite as simple as that. This tree *is* special. It is the fact of it being the 'tree of the knowledge of good and evil' (however one interprets that) which gives it a unique status and importance. But God places limits not because he is a spoilsport but because he is loving. For this tree is the primary means by which the man and woman can express their love and trust in God; it provides the opportunity to disobey him. Without that, these first human beings are little more than programmed robots. When God created life, he never wanted that. He created life for *persons* with whom he could have a relationship and who might relate to one another. It is no accident that immediately after this injunction, God identifies the first 'not good' in his creation: the man's aloneness (Genesis 2:18).

Eden's legal constitution, if we can put it like that, is therefore protective, like so many modern laws. Why else have speed-limits on the roads or officially designated outlets for prescription drugs?

God is clear: eating this fruit is fatal. The snake insinuates that God is scared of them having access to some secret inside information, known only to him. It has all the allure of the conspiracy theorist down the ages, offering access to truth that is concealed from the masses. The snake appeals directly to their prideful ambition and longing for autonomy.

> 'You will not certainly die,' the snake said to the woman. 'For God knows that when you eat from it your eyes will be opened, and you will be like God, knowing good and evil.' (Genesis 3:4–5)

But God's concern was hardly the divulging of secrets. Far from it. He is more like the parent who would never let a ten-year-old sit in the driver's seat while the car engine is running. They are not capable of handling it safely. God's creatures simply lack the capacity to be moral arbiters. Only the Creator truly 'knows' good and evil because only God has the power, wisdom and grace to determine between the two. This is far too lofty an ambition for finite creatures. As proved time after time when we sin. We are too riddled with self-absorption and narrow-mindedness to be morally reliable.

The death that must follow from eating of this tree is both a consequence and a sanction.

The consequence

Death is a consequence because of what eating the fruit represents: rejection of our maker's instructions, our presumption in thinking we know better than the one who wired us for life in his garden. Death for eating from this tree follows as night follows day. Think of one of those old-fashioned deep-sea divers descending to the depths in a huge metal suit. They didn't have compressed gas tanks then. Their only access to air was through long tubes trailed from the surface. Imagine if the diver suddenly decides to do without the air tube, perhaps in the belief that air is not essential. So, he pulls out his diving knife and cuts the tube. It is madness. And fatal – no doubt within seconds. The same is true for the man and woman.

In rejecting their maker's instructions, they are rejecting the maker himself. They are cutting themselves off from the Lord of Life. Of course, death is not immediate, although some interpreters see what happened subsequently as marking a kind of spiritual death. But mortality has now entered into the human experience, and the fact is, Adam and Eve will die eventually.

To articulate this new, tragic reality, Genesis describes the garden's second significant tree, the tree of life (Genesis 2:9). There was no prohibition against eating fruit from this tree. Quite the reverse. It was central to God's grand design for the garden, because the man and woman could live for as long as they had access to it. They could live forever. But once they have disobeyed by eating from the other tree, drastic measures are necessary for the sake of God's entire creation.

The sanction

Notice how God explains the expulsion from the garden.

> The LORD God made garments of skin for Adam and his wife and clothed them. And the LORD God said, 'The man has now become like one of us, knowing good and evil. He must not be allowed to reach out his hand and take also from the tree of life and eat, and live for ever.'
> (Genesis 3:21–2)

In other words, it is now too dangerous. If sinful human beings were immortal, the resulting havoc would be intolerable. What could possibly limit the extent and consequences of human selfishness otherwise? So, this disobedience must be punished, and the man and woman banished. But notice how the trees are mutually exclusive. If you want fruit from the tree of life, you must avoid the tree of the knowledge of good and evil; eat from the tree of the knowledge of good and evil, and your access to the tree of life is forever barred. It has to be this way.

Presumably, access to the tree of life would somehow prevent our inevitable mental decline and physical decay. But after their expulsion, Adam and Eve gradually display the inevitable marks of mortality. That takes time – one explanation for the extraordinarily long lifespans of the first generations after the Fall, perhaps the oddest feature of the Bible's first genealogy in Genesis 5. But don't be distracted by the numbers. Focus, instead, on the chilling refrain echoing through the chapter (with one weird exception in Enoch). It is like a drumbeat of death: 'And then he died... and then he died... and then he died... and then he died... and then he died' (Genesis 5:5, 5:8, 5:11, 5:20, etc.).

This was not part of the creation plan. Death is an alien intruder, but a necessary, inevitable one. Our physical immortality was lost. Adam was made from the dust and to dust we shall return.

Worth: blood for life (Leviticus 17)

the life of a creature is in the blood (Leviticus 17:11)

I have always struggled with most things scientific or mathematical. My initial curiosity gets eclipsed by torrents of chemical formulae, physical properties or impenetrable equations (that some have the audacity to describe as 'beautiful' – I'll never get that). My eyes just glaze over. Give me a rich analysis of a Graham Greene character or Schubert song cycle any day. Still, it isn't necessary to understand all the mechanics to be amazed by something. I haven't the slightest clue about aeronautics or plane design, but I am in awe of huge passenger aircraft. Likewise with human biology. Just ask any medical friends to talk about what amazes or inspires them and it can be very exciting, even when you don't understand every word.

Ancient theories of how the body works can seem unhinged today, but they lacked the benefit of modern, disciplined scientific study. For centuries, doctors believed that we have *two* distinct blood systems, one using veins, the other using arteries. Somehow, the body 'used up' blood, but sickness was caused by an imbalance in the ebb and flow of the two systems. The cure for having 'too much' in one side was therefore 'bloodletting', whereby a patient would have the excess drained off. We know now that this is disastrous and yet it was the practice for over 1,500 years. Change only came with the genius and dogged application of William Hervey among others. Working in seventeenth-century Oxford, he managed to tie together the loose threads of countless others' ideas with his own research. He realised that the body contained not two systems but one, unified system: the same blood circulated throughout the body in what is a truly remarkable biological process.

This means the Bible speaks truer than its human authors could ever have known. In the book of Leviticus, we find instructions that, on first sight, seem very peculiar indeed.

> I will set my face against any Israelite or any foreigner residing among them who eats blood, and I will cut them off from the people. For the life of a creature is in the blood, and I have given it to you to make atonement for yourselves on the altar; it is the blood that makes atonement for one's life. Therefore I say to the Israelites, 'None of you may eat blood, nor may any foreigner residing among you eat blood.'
> (Leviticus 17:10–12)

These instructions may seem strange, and even arbitrary, to us. But the point is not primarily hygienic here, still less dietary. It all revolves around the question of what blood represents: 'the life of a creature'. As commentator Derek Tidball writes:

> The connection between life and blood seems obvious. Loss of blood leads to loss of life – blood shed is life terminated – so it is natural to assume that blood carries the essence of life in it.[14]

Even with sophisticated medical techniques, this principle still stands. How much truer in the ancient world when people lacked basic hygiene, awareness of infection processes and the use of

---

14 Derek Tidball, *The Message of Leviticus: Free to be holy* (Leicester: IVP, 2005).

antibiotics. Even a scratch might prove fatal. So, the sight of blood was ominous indeed. All in all, you were better off only when blood was concealed within the body's veins and arteries. That was easier said than done, of course. Accidents have always happened.

The significance within God's covenant went much further, however. God revealed the intricate system of sacrifices to the people through Moses to make a profound but essentially simple point. Sin is fatal. After all, to reject God's authority over us is to cut ourselves off from the Creator of life. There is a grim logic to that. The only way to deal with the tragedy is to find a way of demonstrating the seriousness of the problem while simultaneously offering an escape route. This is what God offers through atonement. Making us 'one with him' is all his initiative of grace. After all, it's too counter-intuitive for any human being to have come up with this. No human religious system would ever conceive of a system that did not in some way depend on human effort or moral striving. But God, in his mercy, offers a system that requires no striving whatsoever. He offers one life in place of another as a gift. That is what the shed blood points to. The dietary prohibition offers a constant reminder of this. It demonstrates how valuable and precious human life is. After all, he protected the life of Cain with his famous mark, 'so that no one who found him would kill him' (Genesis 4:15), despite the fact that Cain had murdered his brother. Even a murderer's life is valuable. Sin might be fatal, but God longs for a different outcome for sinners. He longs for a way back to life.[15]

This, of course, is precisely what lies at the heart of the gospel. Leviticus can only provide a visual aid, a representation of that gospel. It will take the gift of the greatest life – the bloodshed of God's Son on the cross – to prove quite how precious human life is to God. To do that, however, we will have to grapple with how God squares that with his hatred of human sacrifice.

---

15 This theme is further developed in chapter 8 of Meynell, *Cross-Examined*.

Questions to consider

1 How do human achievements in the biological sciences compare with what God does in creating life? How does this impact our understanding of the meaning and significance of life?
2 Why must God bar the man and woman from access to the tree of life?
3 What evidence do we have for how much value God puts on life?

2

Life not death: the Lord's provision

God himself will provide the lamb (Genesis 22:8)

Tragic folly: Jephthah's vow (Judges 11)

If there's a part of the Bible that young people love the most, it is surely the book of Judges. If it wasn't so full of gruesome stories and nightmare scenarios, it would be easy to recommend it without any qualms whatsoever. Come to think of it, no doubt that's precisely what gives the book its appeal. Few things are more enjoyable for young people than watching adults making complete idiots of themselves. Judges has that in spades. The story of Jephthah is a case in point.

We find ourselves in the most turbulent period of Israel's early history. The nation is fragmented, primarily on tribal lines, which brings with it political chaos. The city states in neighbouring territories constantly agitate for regional dominance, so the people face a seemingly perpetual string of threats from the likes of the Moabites, Canaanites, Amalekites and the Philistines. It is the latter, in alliance with the Ammonites, who cause the most difficulty at the time of Jephthah. Yet, this is not simply the story of regional geopolitics. The writer is explicit about the root causes of Israel's challenges.

> But you have forsaken me and served other gods, so I will no longer save you. Go and cry out to the gods you have chosen. Let them save you when you are in trouble!
> (Judges 10:13–14)

It is impeccable logic. If you are not going to stick with the Lord, why should he stick with you? As happens repeatedly in Judges, however, the people come to their senses eventually and cry out to him for help. Still, the people living around Gilead are at a loss as to who can lead them. How typical of us human beings to come to God only when it is a last resort but then to doubt his ability to bring about change. Cue Jephthah.

Jephthah has had a troubled start in life (Judges 11:1–3), which perhaps explains his impetuous temperament. Despite being the son of Gilead (after whom the territory is named), his mother was not his father's wife but a local prostitute. We never learn her name. Presumably after Gilead has died, Jephthah is unceremoniously booted out by his stepbrothers because, as far as they are concerned, he could claim no part of their inheritance (Judges 11:2). So he leaves, travelling some distance east of the Transjordan Israelite territory. He goes to Tob, which was a settlement roughly situated on the modern Jordan–Syria border. He comes across as one of life's outsiders, socially and psychologically. When his father's family come cap in hand to plead for his assistance – Jephthah's now known as a 'mighty warrior' – it must have been quite a delicious vindication. He certainly milks it for all it's worth, when he asks, 'Didn't you hate me and drive me from my father's house? Why do you come to me now when you're in trouble?' (11:7). Jephthah is not going to risk further rejection and so insists on clear terms before accepting the job.

> The elders of Gilead replied, 'The LORD is our witness; we will certainly do as you say.' So Jephthah went with the elders of Gilead, and the people made him head and commander over them. And he repeated all his words before the LORD in Mizpah.
> (Judges 11:10–11)

That last sentence hints at what is to come. Jephthah clearly appears to want to do the right thing by God. The problem, or perhaps the reason, is that unlike Israel's other 'judges' or leaders, Jephthah was not appointed by God. He was recruited by his relatives, 'the elders of Gilead'. So perhaps he is desperate to compensate for that. Whatever the motivations, things go according to their plans at the start. Jephthah rises to the challenge with a statesmanlike, diplomatic appeal to the Ammonite king (Judges 11:15–27). He uses historical events and territorial claims to make his case, although it should be noted that his account was not entirely accurate; commentators offer various reasons for this, ranging from ignorance to confusion or deliberate deception. Nevertheless, the Ammonite king responds with the condescending hauteur beloved of leaders throughout history: he simply ignores it! 'The king of Ammon, however, paid no attention to the message Jephthah sent him' (Judges 11:28).

There is no way that Jephthah would allow that silence to be the last word. He must act.

> Then the Spirit of the LORD came on Jephthah. He crossed Gilead and Manasseh, passed through Mizpah of Gilead, and from there he advanced against the Ammonites. And Jephthah made a vow to the LORD: 'If you give the Ammonites into my hands, whatever comes out of the door of my house to meet me when I return in triumph from the Ammonites will be the LORD's, and I will sacrifice it as a burnt offering.'
> (Judges 11:29–31)

God is with Jephthah and the people of Israel. He is an insider now, accepted and employed both by his relatives and their God. So far so good. It is at this point that Jephthah makes his catastrophic error, the result of ignorance of God's purposes and character. He makes 'a vow to the LORD'. This is no small matter, no idle pledge. It has all the hallmarks of spiritual devotion. But just reflect for a moment on *what* he promises. He promises to sacrifice 'whatever comes out of the door'. What on earth could he have in mind? Give him the benefit of the doubt and we might imagine a household pet perhaps. But surely, the chances of a person, an actual family member, coming to greet the triumphant hero were just as high? He does seem to countenance the possibility of offering a human sacrifice. As Joseph Hall, the seventeenth-century Bishop of Norwich, observed, 'It was his zeale to vow, it was his sinne to vow rashly.'[1]

Historians give evidence that human sacrifice (even child sacrifice) was a feature of some religious practice in the territories around Israel (as it has been in other parts of the world from time to time), even though it does not seem widespread. So, Jephthah perhaps picked it up from his exile in Tob. What is clear is that if he had known Yahweh and his covenant, he would never have countenanced the idea.[2] While it is only mentioned a few times in the Law, those passages get the point across without any confusion. This is a case in point:

> You must not worship the LORD your God in their way, because in worshipping their gods, they do all kinds of detestable things the LORD hates. They even burn their sons and daughters in the fire as sacrifices to their gods.
> (Deuteronomy 12:31)

If God hates the practice in other religions, why would he endorse it in his own? But as he does consistently throughout this period of the Judges, God delivers his people from their enemies when they turn back to him. That should have been enough to give Jephthah confidence before the battle, without him having to make insane promises as if to twist God's arm. Still, the story is told with agonising pathos, because sure enough, the unbearable happens.

> When Jephthah returned to his home in Mizpah, who should come out to meet him but his daughter, dancing to the sound of tambourines! She was an only child. Except for her he had

---

1 Quoted in Arthur Ernest Cundall and Leon Morris, *Judges and Ruth: An introduction and commentary* (Nottingham: IVP, 2015), p. 142.

2 Yahweh is the anglicised form of the Hebrew revealed name of the God of Israel, YHWH. Since it was regarded in Jewish piety as too holy to utter, *Adonai* (meaning 'Lord') was used in its place. In most modern translations, LORD (wholly in upper case) is used to indicate *Adonai* as a substitute, and Lord (in lower case) for use of the word in its own right.

neither son nor daughter. When he saw her, he tore his clothes and cried, 'Oh no, my daughter! You have brought me down and I am devastated. I have made a vow to the LORD that I cannot break.'
(Judges 11:34–5)

The truth of the matter, however, is that he *could* have broken this vow. Despite the absence of comment from the narrator (there hardly ever is in Old Testament histories), the rest of Scripture leaves us in little doubt that he should have broken it. This was a vow he should never have made in the first place. There would have been some consequences no doubt, but they would surely have been better than losing his only child. Notice how he cannot resist blaming her, of all people. She was the one who 'brought me down' simply because she was the one who walked out of the front door. It's absurd. I can't help wondering why, for example, he didn't tell her (or anyone at home, for that matter) about his vow. Why didn't he get a message back to the household about pushing the cat out first?

It is a tragic story, almost on the lines of ancient drama. In Greek tragedy, a great hero tends to be felled with unerring inevitability because of some deep character flaw. That's true of Jephthah. He is insecure and rash, presumptuous about what God wants of him and yet ignorant of what God has revealed. It is just so sad, not least because his family life had been so dysfunctional at the start. So, I am glad that the biblical writer shows such tender restraint at the end. Jephthah's daughter gets two months' reprieve to spend time with friends and then, 'After the two months, she returned to her father, and he did to her as he had vowed' (Judges 11:39). The less said about that, the better.

Israel may have been rescued from a foreign enemy by Jephthah, but they were embroiled in bitter civil war immediately afterwards. In a particularly cruel and gruesome episode that centred on differences in tribal accents (saying *'sibboleth'* rather than *'shibboleth'* would prove fatal), we are told that the Gileadites killed 'forty-two thousand Ephraimites' (Judges 12:6). Don't assume that just because the writer is silent about these events, he is neutral about them. That is a common mistake with biblical literature. Readers are not meant to approve of what happened, still less are we meant to imitate it. For the law gives us enough. Human sacrifice is never God's plan. He loves life too much. Because he made it.

Which is why the next passage, describing events centuries before Jephthah, is so disturbing. God explicitly commands a child sacrifice.

Tested faith: Abraham's climb (Genesis 22)

Wilfred Owen (1893–1918) was one of Britain's greatest war poets, writing at the same time as a remarkable group of contemporaries like Rupert Brooke, Robert Graves and Siegfried Sassoon. Sassoon became a good friend of Owen's while the two of them were recuperating from shell shock at Edinburgh's Craiglockhart Hospital and it was Sassoon who encouraged Owen's talent. As well as a gifted poet, Owen was also a courageous soldier and awarded the Military Cross in August 1918 (one of Britain's highest awards for bravery). Yet having returned to the front, Owen was killed at the age of only twenty-five. It was only one week before the Armistice formally ended the First World War.

He was steeped in English literature, which meant that he was steeped in the Bible. His poem, 'The Parable of the Old Man and the Young', is the perfect illustration of this. Owen explicitly draws on the account in Genesis 22 of Abraham's weary trudge up the mountain to sacrifice his son. Every educated reader of the time would have known the basic elements of the story. God tells Abraham to take his son, 'your only son whom you love – Isaac' to Moriah where he was to 'sacrifice him as a burnt offering on a mountain that I will show you' (Genesis 22:2). Abraham offers no objection; we are merely told that he embarks on the grim trek with son and servants in tow early the next morning. That is bizarre, because when God revealed that Sodom and Gomorrah were to be judged (Genesis 18:20), Abraham pleaded with him to save the city. Yet, on this occasion, he offers no objections at all. He simply obeys. This is all the more disorientating when we remember the miraculous circumstances of Isaac's birth. God had promised that Abraham would be at the head of a family tree whose members would be numberless like the sand on the shore. The only trouble was that at the time God made this promise, Abraham and his wife Sarah were both elderly and childless. It must have seemed absurd. Yet, sure enough, God eventually performed a miracle and gave them a baby. We could perhaps imagine some confused looks at the hospital reception when Sarah pitches up asking for directions to the Maternity department. 'Surely it's Geriatrics that you need?' says the receptionist to the patient leaning on her Zimmer frame. In fact, when Isaac was born, even Sarah could see the joke.

> Sarah said, 'God has brought me laughter, and everyone who hears about this will laugh with me.' And she added, 'Who would have said to Abraham that Sarah would nurse children? Yet I have borne him a son in his old age.'
> (Genesis 21:6–7)

So, this son – their only child – was to be offered as a burnt sacrifice. It doesn't bear thinking about.

The storytelling is even more poignant than Jephthah's, since we eavesdrop on the fraught conversation between tight-lipped father and baffled son.

> Abraham took the wood for the burnt offering and placed it on his son Isaac, and he himself carried the fire and the knife. As the two of them went on together, Isaac spoke up and said to his father Abraham, 'Father?'
> 'Yes, my son?' Abraham replied.
> 'The fire and wood are here,' Isaac said, 'but where is the lamb for the burnt offering?'
> (Genesis 22:6–7)

Where indeed? Now let Wilfred Owen adapt the account in his own, brilliant way:

So Abram rose, and clave the wood, and went,
And took the fire with him, and a knife.
And as they sojourned both of them together,
Isaac the first-born spake and said, My Father,
Behold the preparations, fire and iron,
But where the lamb for this burnt-offering?
Then Abram bound the youth with belts and straps,
and builded parapets and trenches there,
And stretchèd forth the knife to slay his son.
When lo! an angel called him out of heaven,
Saying, Lay not thy hand upon the lad,
Neither do anything to him. Behold,
A ram, caught in a thicket by its horns;
Offer the Ram of Pride instead of him.

But the old man would not so, but slew his son,
And half the seed of Europe, one by one.[3]

Owen employs shock tactics to drive his point home. Into that final pair of lines, he pours all his rage at the futility and insanity of the war. For there was an alternative to the madness offered by what he calls the 'Ram of Pride'. But the 'old man', representing the senior generation, was apparently content to send Europe's youth to their death, often at a rate of thousands each hour. It is a masterly evocation. But for it to work, the poem's conceit depends entirely on the reader sharing a Bible-shaped revulsion at human sacrifice.

At some point in his thought process, Abraham must have understood this. He knew that the Creator of life itself would never allow for Isaac's execution to be followed through. Not only is life too precious – even that of the fratricidal Cain – but Isaac's life, in particular, was highly significant. God had promised a vast family tree for this elderly, childless couple, and against all odds, they had one son. Isaac was the start of that promise's fulfilment. In the

---

3 Wilfred Owen (1893–1918), 'The Parable of the Old Man and the Young', 1920. Public domain.

Bible's story, this was not simply a matter of the future people of Israel; it is to be the source of God's blessing to the entire world (Genesis 21:12). So, Abraham responds to his son's question.

> Abraham answered, 'God himself will provide the lamb for the burnt offering, my son.' And the two of them went on together.
> (Genesis 22:8)

What happens is heart-stopping. Relief only comes just as Abraham is raising the knife above his son *after having to tie him up*. Only at that very moment, an angel intervenes:

> 'Do not lay a hand on the boy,' he said. 'Do not do anything to him. Now I know that you fear God, because you have not withheld from me your son, your only son.'
> (Genesis 22:12)

Now, at last, Abraham learns the point of this gruesome exercise: to prove he feared God. 'Fear' does not imply abject terror, but healthy awe, wonder, deference, and above all, trust – the only appropriate response of a mortal creature before the eternal Creator. The significance of the moment was not lost on Abraham. He gave the location a name: 'The LORD Will Provide' (Genesis 22:14). Nor was it lost on God. The angel renews his promise of future and global blessing: 'through your offspring all nations on earth will be blessed because you have obeyed me' (Genesis 22:18).

I will never forget a conversation with an American friend when we lived in Uganda. He and his wife had been working in the country for years and had several children of their own. But they encountered a baby in an orphanage who was very sick with life-threatening cardiac problems. They couldn't get him out of their minds. Only one surgical procedure gave him even a remote chance of life, but it was complex and only a handful of hospitals offered it; none were in Africa. Because the boy had no next of kin, it was impossible to travel with him. The only hope was to adopt him, which was a necessarily complex and drawn-out process. There was no guarantee he would live long enough. But then there was the issue of finance because there was no way their health insurance policy would cover the astronomical costs. They booked their flights in faith and prayed. And prayed! For months. Literally a few days before they were due to fly, the adoption papers came through *and* they heard that a hospital in the States would do the surgery for free! My friend said, 'I have learned in life that the Lord is never late, but this episode has taught me that he's rarely early either.' Abraham learned something similar.

Triumphant foreshadowing: Isaac's 'resurrection' (Hebrews 11)

Abraham's experience reverberated down the corridors of biblical history. It became a paradigm for trusting God at moments of confusion and fear. But the surprise is that in the mind of the writer to the Hebrews, the resonance goes deeper. In his so-called 'gallery of faith' in Hebrews 11, in which he explains how faith was fundamental to the spirituality of the great saints of the Old Testament, he writes this:

> By faith Abraham, when God tested him, offered Isaac as a sacrifice. He who had embraced the promises was about to sacrifice his one and only son, even though God had said to him, 'It is through Isaac that your offspring will be reckoned.' Abraham reasoned that God could even raise the dead, and so in a manner of speaking he did receive Isaac back from death. (Hebrews 11:17–19)

In other words, Abraham somehow intuited that even if he went through with the sacrifice of his son, the Lord of Life would restore him to life. He 'could even raise the dead', presumably because such a miracle was easily within the Creator's capacity. Of course, it was unnecessary in this instance, but the logic is striking. It underpins everything we will explore in the rest of this book.

Questions to consider

1 What did Jephthah do wrong (Judges 11)?
2 How is the story of Abraham and Isaac different from Jephthah's?

3

Death's mockery: the impossibility of life?

By any standard, Qin Shi Huang was a titan of world history. He was the first to declare himself Emperor of China, having previously ruled as king, and he reigned as such for eleven more years (221–210 BC). Subsequent generations would portray him as a brutal tyrant and there is certainly truth in that. His territories were vast and subjects almost innumerable. He apparently forced 120,000 families to relocate to his newly established capital city at Xianyang and claimed to have used 700,000 troops to build his mausoleum. Those figures are undoubtedly exaggerated. However, in March 1974, some farmers were digging for wells when they made an astonishing discovery, an archaeological wonder kept secret for over two millennia: the first emperor's burial grounds. It was now clear why its creation demanded such a vast workforce.

Excavation work has so far revealed 6,000 statues arranged in serried ranks, the world-famous terracotta warriors. As well as soldiers, they also represent horses, acrobats and servants, supplied with real chariots, and around 40,000 weapons in bronze and other materials. The emperor's tomb itself has been identified but as yet remains unopened while other zones in its vicinity are worked on (some of which are several kilometres away). There are even thought to be huge palace buildings underground. What prompts a ruler to construct a complex on this scale? It is not pure megalomania, although that is clearly part of it. The answer turns out to be essentially simple, one that is hardly restricted to tyrants: terror of death.

Despite his unprecedented powers, Qin Shi Huang was desperate to overcome humanity's greatest enemy: mortality. He was paranoid about forces conspiring against him, whether human or supernatural, and insisted on maintaining constant secrecy over his location. But security was not his primary concern. As historian Jessica Rawson writes:

> In search of eternal life, the First Emperor urged his officials and associates to seek out herbs and plants that would enable him to evade death and live for ever. Several fruitless expeditions were sent out into the eastern sea to find the mythical islands of Penglai, Yingzhou and Fangzhang, where these plants were believed to flourish. None of these efforts succeeded.[1]

He wanted to live long enough for a cure to death to be found. But if that could not be avoided, what is an eternal sovereign's next best option? Ensure that he has the very best equipment and protection *after* death. In details that seem the stuff of *Indiana Jones* movies, the ancient historian Sima Qian suggests that thousands of craftsmen were deliberately incarcerated when the underground halls were blocked up during the funeral ceremonies; their deaths were deemed entirely fitting. The complex was then threaded with rivers of mercury and crossbows that were primed to fire on any who broke in – all in aid of the emperor's majestic reign beyond the grave.

It is hard not to be reminded of China's first emperor when reading of today's tech billionaires. Their colossal wealth may not have derived from political power but from the canny exploitation of technological ingenuity. But they seem to share some of his instincts. They invest untold millions in medical research, often willing to be their own guinea pigs. Take entrepreneur Bryan Johnson, who made headlines in 2023 by persuading his

---

1   Jessica Rawson, 'The First Emperor's Tomb: The Afterlife Universe' in *The First Emperor: China's terracotta army*, ed. Jane Portal (London: British Museum, 2007).

seventeen-year-old son Talmage to give him a litre of blood while he himself donated a litre to his own father. The exchange took place at a private clinic in Texas, with the ambition of reversing the ageing process, despite the lack of clear scientific corroboration and the strong warnings against the practice by federal authorities.[2] Or take Sam Altman, the CEO of *OpenAI* who has invested $180 million in a biotech start-up called *Retro Biosciences* with the explicit aim of adding a decade to his life.[3] If that seems a lot, then the same article reports that the Saudi government is now keen to invest $1 billion *per year* in the quest for human longevity. These people clearly do not regard this as science fiction. This is obviously not the place to discuss the ethics or science of these attempts; they merely serve to illustrate how, despite passing of millennia and technological improvements, precisely nothing has changed.

The sense of powerlessness before death (Job 9)

Far from being a book for escapists, the Bible consistently confronts difficult or painful reality. The mystery of our mortality is a case in point, and there is no section that probes its depths with greater rigour than the Old Testament's Wisdom literature. Job was a man who lost almost everything (his children, his livelihood, his health) and readers of the book named for him are privileged to eavesdrop on his agonised wrestling, both with his so-called friends or 'comforters' and with God. As Christopher Ash writes

It is a fireball book. It is a staggeringly honest book. It is a book that knows what people actually say and think – not just what they say publicly in church. It knows what people

---

2   Andrea Michelson. 'This Multimillionaire Entrepreneur Infused Himself with Blood from His 17-year-old Son in a Quest to Stay Young Forever', updated 22 May 2023, https://www.insider.com/millionaire-bryan-johnson-swapped-blood-with-teenage-son-young-blood-2023-5, (accessed 5 June 2023).

3   Antonio Regalado, 'Sam Altman Invested $180 Million into a Company Trying to Delay Death', updated 8 March 2023, https://www.technologyreview.com/2023/03/08/1069523/sam-altman-investment-180-million-retro-biosciences-longevity-death/, (accessed 5 June 2023).

say behind closed doors and in whispers, and it knows what we say in our tears.[4]

Job's friend Bildad has insisted that the world runs according to a clear and rigid system (Job 8). According to him, suffering is the universe's punishment for human failure. The more acute a person's suffering, the more heinous their sin. But Job knows – as do we, the book's readers – that he did not deserve what he experiences. As he defends himself ('I am blameless'), his mind ranges wider. He believes that there is a God who is in control of the universe. Yet his experiences push him towards some dark conclusions about God's character.

> Although I am blameless,
>> I have no concern for myself;
>> I despise my own life.
> It is all the same; that is why I say,
>> 'He destroys both the blameless and the wicked.'
> When a scourge brings sudden death,
>> he mocks the despair of the innocent.
> When a land falls into the hands of the wicked,
>> he blindfolds its judges.
>> If it is not he, then who is it?
> (Job 9:21–4)

Death comes to everyone, regardless of the lives they have lived. Job is speaking from bitter experience. In the book's prologue, bandits attack one of Job's properties, killing all but one servant and making off with his livestock (Job 1:14–15). Then, some Chaldeans do precisely the same thing (1:17). To compound the pain, Job's family were enjoying a party at the eldest son's house when a furious storm appears suddenly out of the desert and destroys the building, killing all but one person inside. There were two causes of these horrors: senseless acts of violence on the one hand and

---

4   Christopher Ash, *Job: The wisdom of the cross* (Wheaton, IL: Crossway, 2014), p. 19.

what modern insurance companies still describe as 'acts of God' on the other. Either way, because these people have died, Job cries in despair that it is as if God 'mocks the despair of the innocent'.

So, his question in 9:24 is perfectly logical. If God is not the one in charge and therefore overseeing what happens, 'then who is it?' It was the extremes of his grief over the many deaths that pushed him to the edge. This is because death is the ultimate threat before which all human beings are powerless. There is nothing that anybody can do about it. Now, Job does seem to be aware that he treads on dangerous ground. He cannot quite bring himself to say God brings injustice (that would certainly have enraged Bildad even more). But as Ash comments,

> if he is to hold on to the sovereignty of God, he cannot see what other conclusion he can reach. Who else can act sovereignly on earth? It is a terrible thing that Job says, but we can see why he says it. From his viewpoint it is hard to see what else he can say. There is an honesty about him that is lacking in the comforters.[5]

Job has yet to grapple with the mystery of God having a purpose for suffering in his world. But it is clear that he is confronting the agony of our powerlessness before death. That seems to remain whether one believes in the existence of God or not. It makes little difference. God(s) or no God, in the face of death there is nothing we can do.

The sense of meaninglessness before death (Ecclesiastes 12)

The pilot episode for the hit medical drama *House MD* (starring Hugh Laurie and Robert Sean Leonard) established all the tropes for which it would be justly celebrated. Dr Gregory House is the irascible, misanthropic genius able to cut through sentiment and lies to the life and death issues at stake. He is unwilling to bend to social convention just to make people feel better, preferring to focus on the medical conundrum in the safety of his office than engaging directly

---

5 Ash, *Job*, p. 145.

with people. Having spent most of the episode avoiding one patient, he finally meets her when she refuses the treatment which House is convinced will cure her. Her explanation is her desire for dignity in death. But House is livid, his bedside manner brutal. As far as he is concerned, dignity is only something one can aspire to in life but never when we die. For there is little about death that is remotely dignified, however much contemporary culture tries to whitewash it. We would be hard pressed to deny the truth of his point. Job seems to have understood precisely this when he responds to the news about his family and servants: 'Naked I came from my mother's womb, and naked I shall depart' (Job 1:21). But a lack of dignity at our dying is the least of the problem. In addition to our powerlessness before death, we are confronted with the absurdity of life itself. It takes another Old Testament wisdom book to explore this point: Ecclesiastes, a book by Qohelet, otherwise known as 'The Teacher'.

His is a perplexing book. It teases and provokes, as any rich meditation on the nature of human existence should. After exploring different realms of lived experience, he reaches a startling, poetic summing up. The decay and decline of a person's later years is represented metaphorically. The 'grinders cease because they are few and those looking through the windows grow dim' (Ecclesiastes 12:3, failing teeth and eyes) while, in contrast to the more energetic who wake with the dawn chorus, 'all their songs grow faint' (Ecclesiastes 12:4, failing hearing) and 'the almond tree blossoms' (Ecclesiastes 12:5, silvery hair). The conclusion of the matter?

Remember him – before the silver cord is severed,
    and the golden bowl is broken;
before the pitcher is shattered at the spring,
    and the wheel broken at the well,
and the dust returns to the ground it came from,
    and the spirit returns to God who gave it.

'Meaningless! Meaningless!' says the Teacher.
    'Everything is meaningless!'
(Ecclesiastes 12:6–8)

Life is precious. It is like a silver cord and golden bowl. But it will decay; it will break. The time will come for a last drink of water, after which we return to the dust from which we have all come. This, the inevitable fate of every single one of us, is the reversal of the great miracle of life's creation in Genesis 2:7. Whether we are granted a state funeral that gathers the world's dignitaries or suffer the atrocities of a war crime and get hastily flung into a mass grave, our future is identical. Each of us is destined for compost.

Doesn't this make a mockery of our claims to the value of human life? Whatever our ambitions or achievements, whatever others' memories of us or the legacies we leave behind, all are soon forgotten. As the psalmist rightly reminds us, we are like grass or flowers in a meadow. Then 'the wind blows over it and it is gone, and its place remembers it no more' (Psalm 103:16). It compels us towards the Teacher's cruel verdict: 'Everything is meaningless!' He concludes his book in the same way he opens it (Ecclesiastes 1:2, 12:8). His cry suggests life is something utterly insubstantial. It is empty, brief, forgotten. In fact, the Teacher here echoes Job's description of his own life as but 'a breath' and a vanishing 'cloud' (Job 7:7, 9).

This was precisely the problem that the so-called existentialist philosophers grappled with in the decades after the Second World War. One of the most noted was Jean-Paul Sartre, who articulated his thinking through books like *Nausea*. In this novel, the protagonist, Antoine Roquentin, records in his diary his struggles to find purpose.

> It was true, I had always realized it – I hadn't any 'right' to exist at all. I had appeared by chance, I existed like a stone, a plant, a microbe. My life put out feelers towards small pleasures in every direction. Sometimes it sent out vague signals; at other times I felt nothing more than a harmless buzzing.
>
> I was thinking... that we are here eating and drinking, to preserve our precious existence, and that there's nothing, nothing, absolutely no reason for existing.[6]

---

6 Jean-Paul Sartre, *Nausea*, trans. Lloyd Alexander (New York, NY: New Directions, 1964), pp. 84, 112.

The 'solution', if it can be termed that, is to expend all one's energy fighting against that meaninglessness. But ultimately, it is futile. So perhaps the only thing to do in the face of such futility is to follow the advice of one character in Aldous Huxley's novel *Time Must Have a Stop*.

> Ignore death up to the last moment; then, when it can't be ignored any longer, have yourself squirted full of morphia and shuffle off in a coma.[7]

There is a grim irony here, however. The existentialists were driven to their conclusions by the emptiness of a godless universe. The Teacher was profoundly different, by no means an atheist. His problem was that life seemed utterly devoid of meaning even when God *does* exist. Just as for Job, it was precisely the fact that God reigns supreme that makes these existential problems so painful and perplexing. 'If it is not he [who causes all things to happen], then who is it?' (Job 9:24). But if he is in charge, why can't he do something about this horror?

The answer is, of course, he can. He just seems reluctant for much of the time.

Asking the impossible (Ezekiel 37)

In the years after Israel had suffered the worst thing imaginable – the destruction of the Temple and being dragged thousands of miles away into Babylonian exile – God gives one man an unsettling vision of what he is capable of. It is not the first time he does this for Ezekiel; his first vision had been of the very glory of God, an experience so overwhelming that it left him speechless and housebound for five years (Ezekiel 3:22–6). On another occasion, the prophet is taken to Jerusalem to witness the Israelites' appalling behaviour in the Temple, which precipitated the Lord's glory departing from the Temple as a judgement on it (Ezekiel 8–11). So, what is in store now? Ezekiel is whisked away, perhaps even to the same location as

---

7   Aldous Huxley, *Time Must Have a Stop* (London: Vintage, 2015), p. 212.

that first vision. But instead of seeing God, he is now confronted by 'bones that were very dry', as far as the eye can see (Ezekiel 37:2). It is a gruesome scene, the aftermath of a battle fought weeks before perhaps. The vultures have been and gone, the bare bones glisten in the desert sun. The fact that they lie there out in the open, unburied, even hints that they died under the curse of divine judgement.[8]

God asks the prophet if these bones have any hope of life. Under normal circumstances, that would have been a very stupid question, but Ezekiel is savvy enough to be diplomatic. 'Sovereign LORD, you alone know' (Ezekiel 37:3). He is then given instructions that verge on the grotesque, akin to standing up in an ancient cemetery and holding forth to the gravestones.

> Prophesy to these bones and say to them, 'Dry bones, hear the word of the LORD! This is what the Sovereign LORD says to these bones: I will make breath enter you, and you will come to life. I will attach tendons to you and make flesh come upon you and cover you with skin; I will put breath in you, and you will come to life. Then you will know that I am the LORD.'
> (Ezekiel 37:4–6)

There are deliberate allusions to the Genesis creation account in which lifeless bones are vitalised by God's breath or spirit. But there, the starting point was a body of flesh and blood just waiting to be animated; scattered bones are a very different prospect. However uneasy Ezekiel might have felt about this, he did as he was told.

> So I prophesied as I was commanded. And as I was prophesying, there was a noise, a rattling sound, and the bones came together, bone to bone. I looked, and tendons and flesh appeared on them and skin covered them, but there was no breath in them.

---

8 Christopher J. H. Wright, *The Message of Ezekiel: A new heart and a new spirit* (Leicester: IVP, 2001), p. 304.

> Then he said to me, 'Prophesy to the breath; prophesy, son
> of man, and say to it, "This is what the Sovereign LORD says:
> come, breath, from the four winds and breathe into these
> slain, that they may live." So I prophesied as he commanded
> me, and breath entered them; they came to life and stood up
> on their feet – a vast army.
> (Ezekiel 37:7–10)

The miracle's two-stage process reinforces the Genesis resonance.
The story-teller's details, such as the rattling sound and the newly
invigorated people managing to stand up on their feet unassisted,
serve to make this vision unforgettable. If the army had indeed
been slaughtered and left unburied (as when Babylon swooped
on Jerusalem) as the result of a curse, they are now revived and
restored. God's people could live again to make their stand. If
Ezekiel's very first vision (of God himself) had stunned him and
the second (of the Temple) appalled him, this third vision filled
him with unalloyed hope.

> Then you, my people, will know that I am the LORD, when I
> open your graves and bring you up from them. I will put my
> Spirit in you and you will live, and I will settle you in your
> own land. Then you will know that I the LORD have spoken,
> and I have done it, declares the LORD.
> (Ezekiel 37:13–14)

So, the God of Israel parades his powers before a prophet and his
readers, and it is nothing less than spectacular. Sceptics may retort
that this is no more than a fairy tale, a vision more likely the result
of a narcotic haze than a divine revelation. It proves little. What is
needed are actual miracles.

Witnessing the impossible (1 Kings 17)

Centuries before the tragedies of the exile, however, God had been
at work through another prophet during a time of crisis. Elijah finds
himself commissioned as God's spokesman in the northern kingdom

of Israel (the territory that had broken away from the southern region of Judah after the death of King Solomon) when Ahab is on the throne. This was not a job for the faint-hearted since Ahab and his Sidonian queen Jezebel were determined to wean the people off worshipping Israel's God, Yahweh. Elijah's first task is to predict a devastating, sustained drought. He was then instructed to hide in a ravine where he would be provided with water from a brook and food airlifted in by ravens. When even that brook dried up, he was then sent to a place called Zarephath on the coast, in Jezebel's home region of Sidon. That in itself may have made Elijah a little nervous, though not simply because of the political danger. The standard idea in ancient paganism was for territory to be ruled by whichever gods the people in power worshipped. If your region was conquered, the only sensible thing was to start worshipping your new masters' gods, since your own had clearly been powerless to protect you.

Nevertheless, Elijah heads north and discovers that Yahweh has a plan for him even in enemy territory. A widow has been primed to provide for him even though she and her son have barely enough to live on themselves. Miraculously, her meagre provisions are stretched out because, as God tells her through Elijah, 'The jar of flour will not be used up and the jug of oil will not run dry until the day the LORD sends rain on the land' (1 Kings 17:14). Sure enough, the prophet and his impoverished hosts are spared the extremes of a drought-induced famine. They were not out of danger yet, however. The widow's son sickens and then dies – a personal tragedy with grim repercussions for this woman who is now forced to face old age alone and neglected. She complains to Elijah, 'What do you have against me, man of God? Did you come to remind me of my sin and kill my son?' (1 Kings 17:18). It makes no sense. If God was providing all the food they needed, meagre though it was, to protect them through the drought, how could he have allowed this to happen? So, Elijah takes the boy up to his room and starts pleading with God.

Then he cried out to the LORD, 'LORD my God, have you brought tragedy even on this widow I am staying with, by

45

causing her son to die?' Then he stretched himself out on the boy three times and cried out to the LORD, 'LORD my God, let this boy's life return to him!'
(1 Kings 17:20–1)

The anguish of the scene is palpable. We empathise with this poor mother's agony. We can even understand Elijah's earnest prayers. But it's clutching at straws, isn't it? They are both demonstrating the early stages of grief with their shock and bargaining against the harsh reality of human mortality.

But then the impossible happens.

The LORD heard Elijah's cry, and the boy's life returned to him, and he lived. Elijah picked up the child and carried him down from the room into the house. He gave him to his mother and said, 'Look, your son is alive!'
(1 Kings 17:22–3)

It seems too good to be true. But in her joy, this precious mother draws the only conclusion it is possible to draw: 'Now I know that you are a man of God and that the word of the LORD from your mouth is the truth' (1 Kings 17:24). This miracle has far wider implications than the gladness of one small family, however. For it demonstrates that Yahweh is no prisoner to human boundaries or territories. He is perfectly able to perform the greatest of miracles in the territory of Sidon if he wishes it. That is not all. It emphatically demonstrates that Yahweh is no prisoner to humanity's greatest enemy either. He is not constrained by our mortality, although we should be clear that this young man from Zarephath has only been resuscitated. He will still die one day; he is still mortal. This is no resurrection. Nevertheless, it is no small feat.

A generation later, after Elijah's apprentice Elisha has taken on the mantle, there is another remarkable event. The backstory is that a couple from the town of Shunem show Elisha and his servant Gehazi great hospitality. It transpires that they were unable to have children because the husband was much older than the wife (2 Kings 4:14).

Elisha is able to make a startling promise. 'About this time next year,' Elisha said, 'you will hold a son in your arms' (2 Kings 4:16). It must have seemed the cruellest trick; this was the one thing this woman longed for more than anything. No wonder she responded, 'No, my lord!... Please, man of God, don't mislead your servant!' (2 Kings 4:16). And yet, sure enough, the promise comes true.

As the boy grows up, he is out in the fields and starts screaming about the pain in his head. Was it the heat? A migraine? A haemorrhage? We have no way of knowing. But a few hours later, he dies in his mother's arms. It was all so cruel. Just as the widow at Zarephath had experienced the miracle of being kept alive in a drought only to see her son die, so the Shunammite woman was promised her greatest dream, only to forfeit it so soon after. She turns to the only person she could think of and pleads with Elisha: 'Did I ask you for a son, my lord?... Didn't I tell you, "Don't raise my hopes"?' (2 Kings 4:28). First Elisha sends Gehazi to see if laying his staff on the boy might help. That fails (we are not told why Elisha thought that might work). So, he goes to the family home himself.

> When Elisha reached the house, there was the boy lying dead on his couch. He went in, shut the door on the two of them and prayed to the LORD. Then he got on the bed and lay on the boy, mouth to mouth, eyes to eyes, hands to hands. As he stretched himself out on him, the boy's body grew warm. Elisha turned away and walked back and forth in the room and then got onto the bed and stretched out on him once more. The boy sneezed seven times and opened his eyes.
>
> Elisha summoned Gehazi and said, 'Call the Shunammite.' And he did. When she came, he said, 'Take your son.' She came in, fell at his feet and bowed to the ground. Then she took her son and went out.
> (2 Kings 4:32–7)

It is a very moving scene but also quite comical in its vivid detail. We don't expect a violent sneezing fit as his first waking act. But then, we don't expect corpses suddenly to grow warm.

47

The big questions do not go away, however. If anything, the fact that we have witnessed God doing the impossible through Elijah and Elisha makes us wonder why he doesn't always do it. Why must people die and stay dead?

Questions to consider

1 What is the value of Old Testament Wisdom literature (Job, Psalms, Proverbs, Ecclesiastes, Song of Songs) for Christian believers? How do they help us wrestle with the experience of being mortal?
2 To what extent are Ezekiel's dry bones vision and Elijah or Elisha's miracles an encouragement to trust God? How might they be unhelpful if mishandled?

4

Lifelines: hints of the new life to come

Some ancient myths refuse to die. It's hardly surprising because many are fantastic stories. A case in point is the story of Persephone. Persephone was the stunning daughter of Zeus, king of the gods, and Demeter, the goddess of hunting. One day, Persephone was out in fields collecting flowers with her mother, when suddenly, out of a crack in the ground, leaps Hades, the god of the underworld. He abducts Persephone and drags her down to be his queen. Demeter fruitlessly scours the world for her daughter. Either as punishment for Demeter or because of her grief-stricken neglect, plant life begins to wither away, and humanity slowly starves. But Helios, the sun, sees all and reveals the culprit. The pressure on Hades becomes intolerable, with humanity's cries reaching Zeus and the other gods. Eventually, the kidnapper is forced to relinquish his bride. But because she has been tricked into eating the forbidden food of the dead, she can now never be completely free. As a compromise, Hades lets her out for six months a year. This is clearly an origin story for seasons, with spring and summer the result of her months above ground. Persephone's departure robs the world of its life source and autumn leads inexorably to winter. All is not lost, of course, since spring's miracle of new, resurrected life will accompany her return.

The point is not that people still believe such myths but that they seem historically significant to many. Sir James Frazer, an influential anthropologist a century ago, claimed that certain themes could be traced in the history of all religions, including Christianity, with one of the most prominent being the dying-and-rising god.[1] For Frazer, Persephone and Jesus then fall neatly into the same category. As N. T. Wright notes, there was *something* in it:

> At the heart of the cults was the ritual re-enactment of the death and rebirth of the god, coupled with sundry fertility rites. The productivity of the soil, and of the tribe or nation, was at stake... The myth which accompanied these rituals was indeed the story of resurrection, of new life the other side of death.[2]

There was one crucial difference, however. *Bodily* resurrection simply never featured. What's more, nobody expected the annual cycle of seasons to finish once and for all, as if the 'spring-resurrection' was a newly permanent state of affairs. Persephone rose to die again; Christ emphatically did not. So, there were some parallels with other belief systems – many of them clearly expected some form of existence after the grave (in the underworld, say) or a cycle of death, rebirth and death again (as with the seasons). But people tended to be 'divided into those who said that resurrection couldn't happen, though they might have wanted it to, and those who said they didn't want it to happen, knowing that it couldn't anyway.'[3]

The biblical idea of resurrection was radically new, however. The surprise is that the Old Testament actually hints at it; but before we can see how, we need to grapple with its anticipation of what would happen to Israel's kings. It was never going to be plain sailing.

Long live the King!

The King's suffering is not permanent (Isaiah 53)

All kings suffer. History proves that, even though people can spend their entire lives in its pursuit, a crown brings misery and pain to

---

1   Sir James Frazer was famous for the ground-breaking but controversial book *The Golden Bough*, first published in two volumes in 1890, in three volumes in 1900, and in twelve volumes in 1915.

2   N. T. Wright, *The Resurrection of the Son of God* (London: SPCK, 2003), p. 80.

3   Wright, *The Resurrection of the Son of God*, p. 82.

its wearer. Shakespeare regularly revisited the theme in his plays, creating scores of rulers to populate his worlds. With the constant challenges of rivals and enemies, changing circumstances as well as the competing ambitions of allies, it is little wonder that Henry IV, for example, struggles with insomnia. He confesses, 'Uneasy lies the head that wears a crown' (*Henry IV* Part 2, Act 3, Scene 1). Yet power is its own magnet. Every generation must endure those willing to pay any price to fulfil their craving despite the insecurity and even paranoia that inevitably result.

So far so normal. What nobody expects is the suffering that God's King must also uniquely endure. Isaiah, perhaps more than any of God's Old Testament prophets, had unrestricted access to Judah's royal family. He may even have been related in some way. He famously spoke of a great King descended from David who would wield extraordinary, divine authority (Isaiah 7:10–15; 9:1–7). He also prophesied on several occasions about a mysterious figure called the servant. Sometimes he could be specifically identified. At one moment, he represents God's people Jacob (as in Isaiah 44:1); at another, God's anointed one seems indistinguishable from Cyrus, the pagan king of the Persians (Isaiah 45:1–5). On the whole, he is a kingly figure, one to lead Israel out of her suffering. That is why the extended fourth servant prophecy in Isaiah 52–3 causes the greatest perplexity. This seems to have a very different type of person in mind.

This is not the place for an extended exploration of this Old Testament Mount Everest.[4] We must simply notice how this servant must suffer because 'it was the LORD's will to crush him and cause him to suffer'. The reason is explicit: to make 'his life an offering for sin' (Isaiah 53:10). We have already explored how problematic human sacrifice was through the experiences of Jephthah and Abraham. It was barbaric and explicitly forbidden by Yahweh. Now, the suggestion is that it is somehow Yahweh's will. But it will only begin to make sense once the New Testament confirms that this servant is *also* David's descendant entirely deserving of

---

4 I go into greater depth in chapter 6 in *Cross-Examined*, revised and expanded ed. (London: IVP, 2021).

God's titles and authority; that in Jesus, we encounter both a King and suffering servant who are one and the same. This is morally admissible only because Jesus is God himself. As C. E. B. Cranfield summarises, 'God... purposed to direct against his own very self in the person of his Son the full weight of that righteous wrath which [humanity] deserved.'[5] For this to be effective, the servant cannot simply suffer as if there was something redemptive in suffering in and of itself. His life must be given; he must die if he is to be a 'sin offering'.

At this point, the prophecy becomes truly extraordinary. After this has taken place,

he will see his offspring and prolong his days,
    and the will of the LORD will prosper in his hand.
After he has suffered,
    he will see the light of life and be satisfied;
by his knowledge my righteous servant will justify many,
    and he will bear their iniquities.
(Isaiah 53:10–11)

Yes, this suffering servant will die. But after he has died, he will enjoy 'the light of life' again. The clear implication is that his objective of being a sin offering to 'justify many' and to 'bear their iniquities' has succeeded.[6] The sacrifice has been effective. This King's suffering does not therefore last indefinitely. It was only necessary in so far as it could achieve the remarkable victories of divine forgiveness and grace. Then God grants the servant new life. Taken in isolation, it is hard to know what he has in mind here. Isaiah does not spell out the details. Is the servant resuscitated, only to die again one day? That would be the most normal outcome, the most natural implication of 'prolong his days' after all, such that

---

5   C. E. B. Cranfield, *A Critical and Exegetical Commentary on Romans*, vol. 1, *Romans I–VIII*, 6th ed. (Edinburgh: Clark, 1975), p. 217.

6   The English Standard Version makes the connection between the servant's status before God and those he rescues explicit: 'by his knowledge shall the righteous one, my servant, make many to be accounted righteous' (Isaiah 53:11, ESV).

his life is not as brief as it first seemed. Or is there something more dramatic in view? We cannot decide from this hint alone.

The King is not abandoned to Sheol (Psalm 16)

All kings die. As with contemporary monarchies, so with their ancient predecessors. Even long-lived rulers die, as we in the United Kingdom were reminded in 2022 when Elizabeth II's seventy-year reign ended. The Queen is dead; long live the King! It is unavoidable. A significant number of the psalms are associated with King David, either as the writer or subject matter, or both. So, we would naturally expect some to explore common royal preoc-cupations, especially a king's own mortality or the problem of the succession. Psalm 16 is a fascinating example, one which expresses his confidence in God's sovereignty and personal commitment. This psalm does not seem to be prompted by a particular moment in his life but speaks of God's general provision for all his needs. That is why David is determined to 'keep my eyes always on the LORD [Yahweh]' (Psalm 16:8). This provision fills him with joy, since it operates both in this life and, somewhat unexpectedly, in the next:

> because you will not abandon me to the realm of the dead,
>   nor will you let your faithful one see decay.
> You make known to me the path of life;
>   you will fill me with joy in your presence,
>   with eternal pleasures at your right hand.
> (Psalm 16:10–11)

What on earth can he mean? At the very least, David is confi-dent that the grave will not terminate his relationship with God. Somehow, it will continue. He knows that he will die. The 'realm of the dead' renders the Hebrew word *Sheol*, often simply translated 'the grave', a word more or less equivalent to the ancient concept of the underworld. It is where everybody goes when they die, in a kind of holding pattern. But David is sure he will not be stranded there, nor will he rot. He, 'the faithful one' – in other words, the faithful, anointed King of God's people – will not 'see decay'. Some suggest this is merely confidence that his death will not be premature and so he has plenty of life left to look forward to. However, that seems a rather miserly interpretation. It is much more natural to read it as anticipating benefits *after* death. As such, it does not sound remotely like belief in a cyclical pattern of death and rebirth. Nor even does it resemble a resuscitation. It clearly indicates *new* circumstances, a permanent state unlike anything our world of decay and atrophy has ever known.

The Old Testament tends to be reserved when it comes to realities after death. It is far more preoccupied with this life, focused on the spirituality and ethics of living as God's covenant people in his chosen territory according to the covenant. That does not mean it is silent about such things; only that when it does speak, its statements stand out all the more starkly. No wonder, then, that Peter picks up on these very words in his spine-tingling Pentecost sermon. The twist is his realisation that David was referring not only to himself but also to Christ, the truly faithful one, Great David's Greater Son.

> Seeing what was to come, he spoke of the resurrection of the Messiah, that he was not abandoned to the realm of the dead, nor did his body see decay. God has raised this Jesus to life, and we are all witnesses of it.
> (Acts 2:31–2)

This is not the only occasion on which we find King David's life and poetry anticipating King Jesus'. An even more famous example is Psalm 22 where David describes his own agonies in extraordinary detail, anticipating Christ's passion, and then even his triumph, in uncanny ways. David's assured hope in Psalm 16 is a startling anticipation of the great Messiah's resurrection.

Long live the kingdom!

The Old Testament is like a jumbled-up jigsaw puzzle, with some missing pieces and the rest scattered around the room. It is possible to get a sense of the bigger picture but impossible to grasp every-thing. As faithful Jewish believers tried to put the pieces together, some will have grown in confidence that the story of God's great King in David's line – God's anointed one, the Messiah or Christ – would not end in his death. He would be rewarded with 'the light of life'. But perhaps some wondered how, if at all, this might help *them*. It's all very well for the King but what about his subjects? What difference does that make to us? Help is found in the Bible's Wisdom literature, in the story of Job. It is there that we can see hints of how the king's rewards might be shared with his subjects.

We will see God in our flesh (Job 19)

Job's list of grievances was long and, above all, legitimate. He lost so many of the things that enrich life and make it liveable. Then, while he's desperately clinging to his faith in God, he is driven to the edge by friends who are more concerned with their sense of theological correctness than his pastoral welfare. They want him to acknowledge that he must have done something wrong to bring such punishment on himself. 'How long will you torment me and crush me with words?' he barks back (Job 19:2).

This does not mean Job has correctly interpreted his situation, however. In his desperation of isolation and sickness (he is 'nothing but skin and bones' and has 'escaped only by the skin of my teeth', 19:20), he pleads with the friends.

Have pity on me, my friends, have pity,
    for the hand of God has struck me.
Why do you pursue me as God does?
    Will you never get enough of my flesh?
(Job 19:21–2)

Assuming that God was the one to have struck him is perfectly understandable in his situation, but he is still wrong. Neither he nor the comforters know what we the readers know, namely that Satan (literally, the 'Accuser') had requested the opportunity to test the integrity of Job's trust in God. Christopher Ash explains:

the Satan asks the Lord to 'stretch out your hand'... but the Lord replies, 'Behold, he is in *your* hand.' The hands and fingers that destroyed Job's possessions and killed Job's children and wrecked Job's health were the hands of the Satan, not the hands of God. Yes, it was the hand of the Satan acting with the permission of the Lord and within the strict constraints given by the Lord; but it was the Satan's hand and not God's that actually did these terrible things.[7]

Job longs for relief from the pain and for vindication for what he knew to be true, but there are precious few signs of that happening. And yet it is while his thoughts about God have become very dark indeed that Job is still able to make this astonishing profession of trust:

> I know that my redeemer lives,
>   and that in the end he will stand on the earth.
> And after my skin has been destroyed,
>   yet in my flesh I will see God;
> I myself will see him
>   with my own eyes – I, and not another.
>   How my heart yearns within me!
> (Job 19:25–7)

It sounds a bit like wishful thinking, a daydream, idle talk. But it is surely a statement of confidence – of knowledge, not speculation – which we can only presume is the fruit of divine revelation. God has revealed to him what must happen. Job therefore *knows* that he has a rescuer and that a day will come when Job recognises him.[8] God's King will be seen on earth. What is truly unexpected is Job's personal expectation. He never says this visitation will take place during his lifetime, something which would have made sense even if, perhaps, unlikely. Instead, he claims a hope far more

---

7 Christopher Ash, *Job: The wisdom of the cross* (Wheaton, IL: Crossway, 2014), p. 213.

8 The word 'redeemer' or rescuer in Job 19:25 is the same word that is translated 'kinsman-redeemer' to describe Boaz who helped Ruth (Ruth 2:20).

outlandish. He will encounter him *after* his death ('after my skin has been destroyed'). Just so there is no mistake, he is explicit about what that means. He is not gazing ahead to some ghostly existence beyond the grave, just as even the greatest of Greek heroes had to endure in their underworld. No. He will see his Redeemer 'in my flesh' and 'with his own eyes'. In other words, he will somehow be physically present with his Redeemer. Even though Job still mistakenly believes that God is the cause of his suffering, he has enough faith to trust that he will meet with God and be vindicated. By the end of the whole book, Job's friends are indeed put in their place despite many of his own questions remaining unanswered. But Job does have his sense of God's majesty and sovereignty stretched wide enough to see that he has no right to blame God *for* his suffering but every reason to trust him *through* his suffering.

This must have been hard to live with at times, but it is the way of wisdom and reality. What Job hopes for is nothing less than a resurrection. He has no details of how this happens or what it means. But it is hard to avoid this conclusion: Job believed that the Redeemer would make a resurrection available for those who trust in him. So, if true, it will be possible for people to encounter God beyond the grave, with them somehow physically present with God. They will meet him *in their own flesh.*

We will not be abandoned to Sheol (Psalm 49)

In the Hebrew Bible, what we call Wisdom literature came under the heading of The Writings, and it included the Psalms. It is a natural fit because biblical wisdom deals with all life's realities and enigmas as do these ancient songs. However, Psalm 49 is especially appropriate since its themes might easily have been found in Proverbs or Ecclesiastes. This one is not associated with King David but with the Sons of Korah – a branch of the priestly family of Levi with responsibility for Temple music. In common with the mighty Psalm 73, this psalm wrestles with the age-old conundrum of why the immoral succeed more than those who try to live the good life. So, the poet writes in classic wisdom terms. 'My mouth will speak words of wisdom; the meditation of my heart will give you understanding' (Psalm 49:3).

In the ancient world, wealth was assumed to be a guaranteed sign of divine blessing, in much the same way that Job's comforters assumed that suffering could only mean divine punishment. This is one reason why others tried to keep on good terms with the wealthy in case blessings might overflow on to those close by. The problem was that faithful believers were all too aware how rarely such riches derived from upright practices or devout lifestyles. So, the psalmist corrects their thinking. Life has never worked according to rigid mechanisms that explain away all mysteries. Wicked people grow wealthy, righteous people suffer, accidents and tragedies recur. Is there anything we can be sure of, then? The psalmist offers some stark truths.

> No one can redeem the life of another.
>   or give to God a ransom for them –
> the ransom for a life is costly,
>   no payment is ever enough –
> so that they should live on for ever
>   and not see decay.
> (Psalm 49:7–9)

In other words, no amount of wealth can overcome the ultimate enemy, as if it might be possible to make a payment to God (or take thousands of clay soldiers into the afterlife with you, say, or invest in biotech start-ups) to live forever. Decay is inevitable. As he continues, 'all can see that the wise die, that the foolish and the senseless also perish' (Psalm 49:10). Death is the great leveller. A billionaire may ooze all the effortless sophistication of a jet-set charmer, but in the end, 'People, despite their wealth, do not endure; they are like the beasts that perish' (Psalm 49:12). It is a cruel fact of our mortality that we are reduced to the status of the farmyard or forest animal. Then for the wealthy, they must face the fact that 'Their forms will decay in the grave, far from their princely mansions' (Psalm 49:14).

The psalmist now makes a dramatic pivot.

But God will redeem me from the realm of the dead;
   he will surely take me to himself.
(Psalm 49:15)

Note the tense of the verb. 'God *will* redeem me,' he says. The grave makes worldly wealth meaningless and impotent; 'no one can redeem the life of another', he said in verse 8. That is true. But when Jesus confronted a rich man's religious entitlement and conceit (which prompted him to leave depressed), he reassured his disciples. 'What is impossible for man is possible for God' (Luke 18:27). A human being may not be able to redeem a life or live a good enough life for God. But God can.

The psalmist is speaking of Sheol, the place where the dead are gathered. It is from there that God will rescue him and 'take him to himself'. It is very similar to Job's hope. It is for life after the descent into the grave. There is no suggestion of anything cyclical here. Nor any sense that this is something exclusively reserved for the king. This is an ordinary believer's expectation. Just like the king, he is sure that he will not be abandoned to Sheol.

Taken individually, these verses may seem slight and insignificant. They are no more than hints and we would certainly be unable to construct a full understanding of resurrected life from them alone. But once the jigsaw pieces are brought together and understood through a New Testament lens, it is clear they point unequivocally towards something glorious, real and available. Even for the likes of us. This is not the stuff of legend, still less of wishful thinking. This is the stuff of a victory won by a man in time, and space and in human history. To that we now at last turn.

Questions to consider

1 In what ways is the Old Testament like an incomplete jigsaw puzzle?
2 What sets Old Testament expectations for what happens after death apart from other belief systems and worldviews around today?

Part 2

PRESENT: SPIRIT ALIVE

From the very start, the Gospel writers present Jesus as God's King who will 'save his people from their sins' (Matthew 1:21). Jesus' fulfilment of Old Testament expectations for new life put death in its place. After his death, burial and resurrection, he is finally declared to be God's King who reigns over everything. What he achieved for himself by rising is then promised to all who ally themselves with their King.

5

Death's impotence: Jesus could not be contained

A delicious story is told of a conversation in 1972 between the Chinese Premier, Zhou Enlai and America's then National Security Advisor, Henry Kissinger. To a question about his thoughts on the French Revolution, Zhou replied, 'It is too early to say.' Almost immediately, this phrase became emblematic of China's reputation for taking long-term views on world events. Even so, that seemed to stretch things a little too far. After all, the French Revolution had taken place two centuries before resulting in innumerable reverberations, one of which had been China's own communist revolution. The truth about the conversation is rather more mundane. One diplomat present at the meeting later explained that Zhou had misunderstood Kissinger and assumed he was referring to the Parisian student protests of 1968. The mistake was understandable, because many of the students explicitly claimed to be following in the footsteps of the revolutionaries of 1789 to explain their protests.[1] Zhou was making a simple point. It was impossible to determine the significance of the protests, if any, less than five years on. The more shocking the event, the harder it is to interpret. If that was true of something quickly forgotten like the Paris protests, how much more is it of an event as seismic as Jesus' resurrection.

On the first Easter Sunday, the tomb was empty. That much was true. If it had not been empty, there is no way the rumours about a risen Jesus would have started. It was precisely what the

---

1   Tyler Cowen, '"It Is Too Soon to Tell": the Real Story China Fact of the Day', *WMU*, updated 11 June 2011, https://marginalrevolution.com/marginalrevolution/2011/06/it-is-too-soon-to-tell-the-real-story.html, (accessed 9 June 2023).

authorities were desperate to avoid (Matthew 27:62–6). Nor would there have been rumours had Jesus' friends simply turned up at the wrong tomb. It would have been straightforward for the authorities to produce a body. The persistence of rumours must mean that nobody did so. So, if the correct tomb was indeed empty, the question is obvious: What had happened to the body? It would have taken a few hours to figure that out. But it would take months, and indeed years, for those first believers to figure out what it all meant.

One common mistake here is to assume that the resurrection proves Jesus must be the Messiah or divine. That is not quite right. As we have already noted, the Bible describes several 'raisings', through Elijah and Elisha in the Old Testament and then through Jesus and the apostles in the New Testament.[2] These were special events to be sure. But nobody started drawing conclusions about those now seen wandering around. Another point is often missed about the two who famously left Jerusalem on the Emmaus Road. They are perplexed and confused, apparently despairing that they could no longer accept what they once believed about Jesus, namely 'that he was the one who was going to redeem Israel' (Luke 24:21). The surprise is they leave even *after* hearing about the tomb.

> They went to the tomb early this morning but didn't find his body. They came and told us that they had seen a vision of angels, who said he was alive. Then some of our companions went to the tomb and found it just as the women had said, but they did not see Jesus.
> (Luke 24:22–4)

Even news as odd as that wasn't enough to keep them in town. They must have been mystified about what had happened exactly, but the possibility of Jesus being alive again seemed remote. Even the most loyal and faithful of his disciples were going to need much more to convince them of that. It was simply too soon. Jesus had

---

2 The Nain widow's son (Luke 7:11–17); Jairus's daughter (Luke 8:49–56); Lazarus (John 11); Tabitha through Peter (Acts 9:36–42); Eutychus through Paul (Acts 20:7–12).

predicted his rising.[3] But it is highly unlikely that it registered, what with the emotional maelstrom of discovering that Jesus expected to suffer, quite apart from the sheer implausibility of resurrection. On first hearing, any sane person would dismiss such a prediction as deranged. And even if it had registered, nobody understood it as Jesus intended. As N. T. Wright and others have forcefully argued, *nobody* was expecting Jesus to be raised bodily.[4]

It would take weeks for the implications to sink in. In particular, it would require time in the presence of the risen Jesus. Luke opens his second volume with a snapshot of the period between Easter and Pentecost, explaining that:

> After his suffering, he presented himself to them and gave many convincing proofs that he was alive. He appeared to them over a period of forty days and spoke about the kingdom of God.
> (Acts 1:3)

It must have been an unforgettable few weeks. Oh, to have been a fly on the wall! But notice how Luke describes Jesus giving 'convincing proofs' that he was alive. No wonder! It was all so unlikely. By the time their time with Jesus came to an end, the disciples were primed, ready for the final piece of God's mission jigsaw: the pouring out of the Holy Spirit at Pentecost. He would give them all the power and courage needed to take news of Jesus' Easter revolution to the world (Acts 1:8). This explains the rich brilliance of Peter's Pentecost sermon (Acts 2:14–39). He says surprisingly little about the Holy Spirit but radiates wonder at the risen Jesus. They didn't need *proof* of Jesus' resurrected life now; they simply had to pass on what they had witnessed and learned (Acts 2:32), and that is exactly what Peter does.

While there are many fascinating details in the sermon, one verse provides an especially useful entry point into what it all

---

3 See, for example, Mark 8:31, 9:31 and 10:33–4.
4 N. T. Wright, *The Resurrection of the Son of God* (London: SPCK, 2003), p. 578.

means: 'But God raised him from the dead, freeing him from the agony of death, because it was impossible for death to keep its hold on him' (Acts 2:24).

Peter's language here is startling but hard to capture in translation. The word for 'agony' normally has a very specific context: a mother's excruciating pain in childbirth.[5] That is appropriate for conveying the intensity and trauma of the cross. However, it is odd to apply it to death itself, rather than dying. Peter is mixing his metaphors in an ingenious way. By definition, death is normally an end. But Jesus transforms it. Death is now like a mother's pains: intense but not indefinite, the fearful but necessary phase before a new life arrives. Like a newborn child, Jesus could not be held back. Peter implies that the resurrection is inevitable – 'it was impossible for death to keep its hold on him' (Acts 2:24).

Peter's statement is strange, to say the least. It is hard to think of anyone else in human history that it could possibly have been applied to. The obvious question is, why couldn't it keep hold of him? What was it about Jesus' life and ministry that made it so impossible? We will explore several connected aspects of this which hold together rather like different facets of a brilliant diamond.

...because of Jesus' promises to rise

As we have seen, returning from the grave is insufficient proof in itself for Jesus' claims to be heaven-sent Messiah. It is his resurrection promises and predictions that make the difference.

Imagine that I run out into the high street and get knocked down by the number 63 bus. Hopefully, you would think that a shame and that I'd be missed. If after a few days I managed to wake up and slide open the mortuary body drawers, you would be delighted to have me back, I'm sure. So far, so happy. But what if I'd been predicting for months that this would happen? Now, of course, bus timetables and careful planning could have made the circumstances of my demise easily predictable. But that's not the tricky part. Far harder to pull off is the rising-from-the-dead part.

---

5   The word is *tas ōdinas*, literally 'birth pains' (as used in 1 Thessalonians 5:3).

Get *that* bit right, then suddenly everything else I said or did is cast in a very different light. That is all quite absurd, of course. But not with Jesus. It is precisely what happened.

Mark structures the second half of his Gospel in a fascinating way. The book hinges on a stunning moment in Caesarea Philippi, where Peter publicly recognises Jesus' identity for the first time. 'You are the Messiah' – the Christ, God's King' (Mark 8:29). This is immediately followed by a move that must count as one of Jesus' oddest. 'Jesus warned them not to tell anyone about him' (Mark 8:30). Jesus doesn't rebuke or correct Peter's answer. Instead, he insists that his follower keeps his discovery to himself. As he unfolds the story, though, Jesus knows exactly what he is doing. The reason is that the world was not yet ready. Everybody assumed they knew what kings were like. Nobody could yet grasp what it meant for *Jesus* to be King.

> He then began to teach them that the Son of Man must suffer many things and be rejected by the elders, the chief priests and the teachers of the law, and that he must be killed and after three days rise again.
> (Mark 8:31)

As if proof were needed of the world's unpreparedness, Peter wades straight in to dissuade Jesus. The result was a moment that must have chilled him for the rest of his life. Jesus rebukes him as 'Satan', since only Satan could want Jesus to avoid the cross (Mark 8:32–3). Jesus is saying that it *must* be like this for the Son of Man (his favourite description of himself). He must go to the cross. But he must also rise. It is predicted and promised.

Mark has Jesus repeating it twice, each time with a little more detail.

> He said to them, 'The Son of Man is going to be delivered into the hands of men. They will kill him, and after three days he will rise.' But they did not understand what he meant and were afraid to ask him about it.
> (Mark 9:31–2)

After Peter's experience, no wonder they were reluctant to question him. Jesus explains again:

> 'We are going up to Jerusalem,' he said, 'and the Son of Man will be delivered over to the chief priests and the teachers of the law. They will condemn him to death and will hand him over to the Gentiles, who will mock him and spit on him, flog him and kill him. Three days later he will rise.'
> (Mark 10:33–4)

These are Jesus' most explicit predictions, but we find other occasions when he clearly has this in mind. Take the strange connection he made to the prophet Jonah, sent to preach to the Assyrian capital city, Nineveh: 'For as Jonah was three days and three nights in the belly of a huge fish, so the Son of Man will be three days and three nights in the heart of the earth' (Matthew 12:40). To which, Jesus asserts that 'something greater than Jonah is here' (Matthew 12:41). After all, a resurrection is undoubtedly 'greater' and more remarkable than being vomited out of a whale.

A resurrection is also more remarkable than King Herod's reconstruction of the Temple. Jesus claims to be 'one greater than the temple' (Matthew 12:6) because, as John records, he said, 'Destroy this temple, and I will raise it again in three days' (John 2:19). Nobody at the time understands – the disciples included – because they take him literally. It only began to make sense after that first Easter Sunday (John 2:20–2). Jesus clearly expects it to happen, which is why he predicts it.

We need to go further, however, because promises and predictions do not get to the heart of *why* death could not keep hold of him. For that, we need to delve into Christianity's most mysterious corners and into the very identity of Christ.

…because of Jesus' identity

• …*as God*
The early church spent decades coming to terms with what the first disciples witnessed and passed on. That things got complicated

should come as no surprise. At the heart of the Christian message is the idea that an eternal and infinite God steps into the finite world he had made; the Creator becomes a creature. Trying to articulate in human language how this all worked is bound to be complicated. So even though words like Trinity and Incarnation are not found in the Bible (much to sceptics' glee), it is important to grasp how they came about.

With the foundations and limits set by the Scriptures, the first generations of Christians used a process of theorising and debate. Figuring out how to hold everything together must have felt like trial and error at times. Someone would offer an idea or concept after which the Church would sit with it for a time, stress-testing it, much like an engineer does with a revolutionary new design.

A case in point is Christology, the study of Jesus' identity. Theologians meditated long and hard about what the Bible teaches. They agreed that Jesus must be *fully* human: he experienced all of life's ups and downs, physically and psychologically. Then, in what could be described as his most human moment, he died. There was no sleight of hand or fakery. He genuinely did die. The length of time he would stay in the tomb indicated that: too long for someone to be able to wake from a 'swoon' (as some claim), too long for a corpse to avoid decomposition. But insisting that Jesus was fully human hardly says much. Jesus was so much more. While few would have guessed it on first meeting, believers realised that prolonged contact made one conclusion inescapable: he must also be *fully* divine. He had mastery over all creation including the elements (he calmed storms, healed diseases and fed thousands out of someone's lunch box). He had authority over the spiritual realms (he expelled demonic powers) as well as over human affairs (just consider who is in control when he gives opponents the slip or during his various trials). He spoke and taught with an authority that had never previously been witnessed. Finally, he did not stay dead. Put all the jigsaw pieces together and only one thing makes sense. He is fully God. How else to make sense of a claim like this one being true?

> The reason my Father loves me is that I lay down my life –
> only to take it up again. No one takes it from me, but I lay it
> down of my own accord. I have authority to lay it down and
> authority to take it up again. This command I received from
> my Father.
> (John 10:17–18)

And the point is this: only God could be in control of both his own
death *and* his return from death.

The problem now is how on earth to hold the human and divine
together. It is quite the brainteaser because it appears to make little
sense, especially if we try to imagine it physically. We all know
that it is impossible for two people or objects to occupy the same
space at the same time. So, we might naturally assume that for
Jesus, he cannot be both fully human and fully God. One aspect
must somehow cancel out or displace the other. But this is where
thinkers made an important distinction: between a person and his
or her nature.

Imagine you and a friend take the dog for a walk in the park. It
is that strange time after sunset when the light is dim, but you can
still glimpse just enough through the gloom to avoid accidents. You
spot a rough shape moving around up ahead in the distance. If you
cannot identify it, you might ask, 'What is that?' That is a question
about its nature: is it animal, vegetable or mineral? As it comes closer,
you realise that the shape is in fact a person. She is a human being.
But if you cannot identify her, you now ask, 'Who is that?' That is
a question about the individual person. Because of her nature as a
human being, she has certain capacities. You know that in normal
circumstances, she is able to walk and talk, breathe and laugh; but
she is unable to fly or read minds. Because of her personhood, she
has a personality, which means she might find only certain jokes
funny or avoid some circumstances as stressful. This gives us a way in
to understanding what it means for God to become a human being.

The difference with Jesus is that his uniqueness could only be
explained if he had *two natures* simultaneously. He was always
one person. He was not divided or somehow schizophrenic; he

was fully integrated in himself. But he had two natures. Does this matter? Yes! Because of his human nature, he had the capacity to live and die on earth. Because of his divine nature, he had the capacity to defeat death and rise again. In fact, because of his divine nature, he *could not* die. His divine nature could not let his human nature stay dead. Thus, death could not keep a hold on him. He *had* to rise. Of course, this explanation took time to be clarified because people could only encounter Jesus as an individual person. As the disciples huddled in the upper room waiting for Jesus' instructions, they could never have figured all this out at once. All they knew was that they had met Jesus again.

● *...as the Messiah*
We have already touched on another aspect of Jesus' identity that is relevant for understanding the resurrection: the Old Testament expectations for the new Messiah. This is central to Peter's argument at Pentecost. Everyone in Jerusalem knew that David had been king and had then died: 'his tomb is here to this day' (Acts 2:29). If that is the case, then, who can David be referring to in Psalm 16 (as we considered in the previous chapter)? It cannot be David himself, since he *had been* 'abandoned to Sheol'. It makes more sense to see David anticipating a descendant, one whom Isaiah would also, in time, predict.

> But he was a prophet and knew that God had promised him on oath that he would place one of his descendants on his throne. Seeing what was to come, the spoke of the resurrection of the Messiah, that he was not abandoned to the realm of the dead, nor did his body see decay. God has raised this Jesus to life, and we are all witnesses of it.
> (Acts 2:30–2)

So, the resurrection had to happen because of God's ancient promises as well as those of Jesus during his own lifetime.

As a result, the resurrection unequivocally proves Jesus' credentials. He genuinely is the Messiah, great David's greater heir and successor. Peter had been exactly right at Caesarea Philippi. He is the Christ before whom all Israel should bow. The resurrection did not qualify Jesus to become the Messiah. The resurrection had to take place because he already was, and always had been, the Messiah.

...because of Jesus' sacrifice for sin

It often goes unremarked, but Jesus' final cry from the cross also echoes his ancestor, David. When he gasps, 'It is finished' (John 19:30), he in fact alludes to the same psalm he had quoted moments earlier: Psalm 22. It is an astonishing prayer, written when David was facing extreme anguish. But while we can take much of what David wrote as metaphorical depictions of his own experience, it finds actual fulfilment centuries later in Jesus' final hours. When David cries out in fear and confusion at the start of the psalm – 'My God, my God, why have you forsaken me?' (22:1) – he puts what he feels into words. As God's chosen king of Israel, he was not forsaken. But when Jesus quotes David's words from the cross, he genuinely was (see Table 1 for a comparison of David's experience with that of Jesus).

Jesus experiences what it means to be cut off from God as a sanction for sin, the just consequence for rejecting God. Or as Paul would later write, 'the wages of sin is death' (Romans 6:23). Jesus suffers in the most horrendous ways – physically, psychologically, spiritually. Psalm 22 barely scratches the surface of it, accurate though it undoubtedly was. And yet... David does not leave us in the pit of despair. The tone and focus change radically in verse 19, with renewed confidence in God's saving power, and, even more remarkably, in ultimate, public vindication. The whole world and all generations to come will find out about this (22:27). Why? Presumably, because the cry of God's afflicted one was heard (22:24) and his mission was accomplished. 'They will proclaim his righteousness, declaring to a people yet unborn: He has done it!' (Psalm 22:31).

David does not tell us explicitly what that mission was. It is simply another piece in the Old Testament jigsaw. By the time we get to Jesus, it is clear. Matthew tells us that Mary was instructed

Table 1 Suffering Christs

The Christ David (Psalm 22)	The Christ Jesus (in the New Testament)
Feeling abandoned *My God, my God, why have you forsaken me? (22:1).*	Being abandoned *Why have you forsaken me? (Matthew 27:46).*
Rejected *Scorned, despised, mocked: He trusts in the* Lord, *let the* Lord *rescue him (22:6–8).*	Rejected *Let the Lord rescue (Matthew 27:42–4).*
Alone *Do not be far from me, for trouble is near and there is no one to help (22:11).*	Alone *Arrested in Gethsemane (Matthew 26:42–6).*
Humiliated *All my bones are on display; people stare and gloat over me. They divide my clothes among them and cast lots for my garments (22:17–18).*	Humiliated *Stripped and mocked (Matthew 27:27–32). Casting lots (Matthew 27:34–5).*
Eventually honoured *All the ends of the earth will remember and turn to the* Lord, *and all the families of the nations will bow down before him (22:27).*	Eventually honoured *All peoples of the earth (Matthew 24:30, 26:64). Every knee will bow (Philippians 2:6–11).*
Mission accomplished *They will proclaim his righteousness, declaring to a people yet unborn: He has done it! (22:31).*	Mission accomplished *It is finished (John 19:30).*

to name him Jesus 'because he will save his people from their sins' (Matthew 1:21). Jesus is the Greek form of Joshua which means 'the Lord saves'. This sets the agenda for the whole of Matthew's Gospel. So, if we fast forward to the very end of the book, it helps us to explain what happens on the cross. Once he took his last breath, 'the curtain of the temple was torn in two from top to bottom' (Matthew 27:51). The symbolism is unmistakable. The Temple represented everything that barred us from the presence of a Holy God. But now the barrier has been torn down. That is something only God could achieve (hence the detail of being dismantled from top to bottom). So even though Matthew does not include the final cry that John quotes, he effectively declares the same thing. Each of the four Gospels is clear. Jesus has accomplished what he came to do... by dying on the cross.

This means that there is nothing left for Christ to do for sinners. There is nothing left to punish him for. No wonder death could no longer keep its hold on him.

...because of Jesus' victory over Satan

Around the time the Israelites were sent to Babylon in exile (the sixth century BC), there apparently lived a brilliant military strategist on the other side of the world by the name of Sun Tzu. While some doubt his existence, the same cannot be said for the book associated with him: *The Art of War*. This ancient Chinese text has wielded global influence, because of its pithy proverbs about gaining military victories. Here are some examples:

He will win who knows when to fight and when not to fight... He will win who, prepared himself, waits to take the enemy unprepared.

O divine art of subtlety and secrecy! Through you we learn to be invisible, through you, inaudible; and hence we can hold the enemy's fate in our hands.

Let your plans be dark and impenetrable as night, and when you move, fall like a thunderbolt.[6]

Jesus never read Sun Tzu, of that I'm sure. Yet he does seem instinctively to have appreciated his tactics. He was engaged in a cosmic war, the like of which the world had never witnessed: the ultimate battle of good vs evil, with the Son of God up against that fallen

---

6   Sun Tzu, *The Art of War*, trans. Lionel Giles (Atlanta, GA: Dalmatian Press, 2007), pp. 31, 39, 41.

angel, the great deceiver and father of lies himself. From even before the beginning of time, the devil was determined to ruin everything that God did. The mistake is to imagine an even match, as if there were days when Jesus was on top and days when Satan was. There is not the slightest hint of this in the New Testament. Christians are not dualists. But we might begin to think so because the tactics of the two sides were so different. This is most apparent at the point early in Jesus' public ministry when the war comes out into the open. This was not the war's final phase, but it did mark its most decisive battle. Yet Satan's tactics were so confused. One moment, he goes out of his way to prevent Jesus from going to the cross; the next moment he actively orchestrates Jesus' downfall.

Satan diverts Jesus from the cross

Even if not explicitly mentioned, Satan beavers away throughout the story of the incarnation to disrupt and thwart. He is undoubtedly behind King Herod's homicidal rage in Bethlehem after Jesus is born (Matthew 2:16). But his tactics become overt when Jesus goes into the desert (Luke 4:2–13 or Matthew 4:1–11). The temptations are unexpected, to say the least. Suggesting that the starving Jesus turn stones to bread is perhaps understandable, and the offer of the kingdoms of the world is at least alluring; but the opportunity to fling himself off the Temple roof is truly bizarre. What is going on here? The key is to see Satan as attempting to wrest Jesus away from his Father's influence and authority (much as had happened to Adam and Eve in the Garden). Satan is usurping the Creator.

Will Jesus trust the Father to sustain him in the desert or use a quick-fix food miracle to prove his credentials as Son of Man? (Luke 4:3). Time would show that Jesus was perfectly capable of such wonders when he fed five thousand (Luke 9:10–17). But he had no need to prove himself to anyone at this stage, least of all the devil.

Will Jesus worship the devil in exchange for the all the kingdoms of the world? (Luke 4:5–7). Satan claims they are his and that he 'can give them to anyone he wants to.' He is not entirely wrong; he is called the 'prince of this world' in John's Gospel, for example. He dangles his worldly baubles and enticements to attract worshippers. Nobody would fall for it otherwise. The catch is that none of them are permanent. Satan's reach is confined to 'this world'.

Will Jesus launch his global campaign with a spectacular debut at the centre of the Jewish world? What could be more dramatic than getting scooped up by a battalion of angelic rescuers? (Luke 2:9–11). It would be a PR consultant's dream.

Jesus is measured in his response. He merely quotes the Bible back at Satan (despite the latter having attempted to lure him with verses), drawing from two chapters: Deuteronomy 6 and 8. These are entirely apt since they contain Moses' preaching to the generation of Israelites about to enter the Promised Land, urging them to heed the lessons of their parents' desert wanderings. They are to remain loyal to their rescuer God, come what may. But it is not simply Jesus' loyalty that Satan is trying to steal. He is offering him an alternative mission, one that avoids suffering: a shortcut to comfort, protection and global dominance, without the cross. There is just one snag: it involves worshipping the devil. That is not remotely an option, even though in Gethsemane, Jesus feels the agony of his resolve acutely. It is intriguing, however, that Satan wants to divert Jesus from the cross, presumably on the logic that if it is God's plan, he must thwart it.

This must be why Jesus reacts with such apparent violence to Peter's quiet concern in Mark 8. We naturally sympathise with Peter's attempt to dissuade Jesus from going to his early death and are shocked by Jesus' reaction: 'Get behind me, Satan! You do not have in mind the concerns of God, but merely human concerns' (Mark 8:33). Yet this fits perfectly with what Jesus experienced in the wilderness. But when we stop to think about it, this is very strange. Why *wouldn't* Satan want Jesus to be executed? Especially since, at times, this is precisely his plan.

Satan drives Jesus to the cross

From the start, Jesus encounters all manner of interference and nuisance tactics. As his reputation spreads, religious leaders understandably want to check him out. It is quickly apparent that they are not neutral enquirers since, in Mark's account, they immediately draw the darkest of conclusions: he is a blasphemer – a capital sin (Mark 2:6–7). They keep track of him and complain about the quality of people he associates with, his team's lack of fasting, and Sabbath disobedience (Mark 2:16, 18, 24) Then, after the scandal of healing on the Sabbath, they have had enough.

> Then the Pharisees went out and began to plot with the Herodians how they might kill Jesus.
> (Mark 3:6)

Notice how early in Jesus' public ministry this is. They want him dead almost from the outset. What else could make such bitter enemies find a common cause? The Pharisees were first-century equivalents of biblical fundamentalists and the Herodians compromising prag-matists willing to work with Rome's client king. It is not unreasonable to suppose that a dark force was at work behind this.

The leaders are not the only ones disturbed by Jesus. Even his own family are troubled. 'He is out of his mind,' they say (Mark 3:21). Then in the grimmest of ironies, some Pharisees have the audacity to accuse Jesus of being in league with the devil: 'he is possessed by Beelzebul! By the prince of demons he is driving out demons' (Mark 3:22). That is absurd, as Jesus proves (Mark 3:24–30).

Jesus is under no illusions. His disciples must have found it hard to grasp why anybody would reject him, but he knows there are many trip hazards on the road to trusting him. That is what prompts one of his most famous parables – of the sower and the soils. Jesus explains:

> Some people are like seed along the path, where the word is sown. As soon as they hear it, Satan comes and takes away the word that was sown in them.
> (Mark 4:15)

The devil is determined to undermine the impact of Jesus' preaching. But it is not until the end of Jesus' ministry that the devil's handiwork is completely unmasked. We might speculate which formed the most heart-breaking moments of his final hours, but two of the worst must have been the betrayals by Judas and Simon Peter. We read in Luke's account that Satan was involved in both. Before he made a deal to the religious leaders with a deal to hand Jesus over, we are told that, 'Then Satan entered Judas, called Iscariot, one of the Twelve' (Luke 22:3). Jesus knows exactly what is going on, which must have been devastating for Judas. By voicing his awareness, it is almost as if Jesus is telling him that he doesn't need to do this.

> But the hand of him who is going to betray me is with mine on the table. The Son of Man will go as it has been decreed. But woe to that man who betrays him!
> (Luke 22:21–2)

Then, in anticipation of Peter's well-intentioned but misplaced bravado, Jesus tells him:

> Simon, Simon, Satan has asked to sift all of you as wheat. But I have prayed for you, Simon, that your faith may not fail. And when you have turned back, strengthen your brothers.
> (Luke 22:31–2)

Peter will not have the courage to admit even to being an acquaintance of Jesus on that darkest of nights. But here, Jesus shows exquisite pastoral concern. Unlike Judas, Peter has a future here, even though he also is afflicted by Satan's schemes. For, unlike Judas, Peter is prepared to face his failures and turn back to Jesus for forgiveness.

Satan wants Jesus betrayed, he wants him isolated, he wants him dead. And he achieves all three. Such is the revenge of the scorned bully rejected by Jesus in the desert. As Jesus is brutalised by soldiers, dragged to and from kangaroo courts and cowardly administrators, then executed on the most appalling instrument of torture available, Satan was indeed winning. The cosmic battle was over. God's Christ was defeated.

Until he wasn't.

For those who could remember it, Jesus' encouragement to followers sent out on an early training mission would have been a great comfort: 'I saw Satan fall like lightning from heaven' (Luke 10:18). When the seventy-two were ministering in those villages on their mission, they had achieved wonders. As they did so, Jesus saw Satan defeated. This anticipated his final defeat. Any enemy smugness on Good Friday evaporated by Easter Sunday. On that day, as Paul would write, 'Death has been swallowed up in victory' (1 Corinthians 15:54). Jesus had died but then defeated death; he would never die again: 'death no longer has mastery over him' (Romans 6:9). C. S. Lewis sums it up perfectly:

> The New Testament writers speak as if Christ's achievement in rising from the dead was the first event of its kind in the whole history of the universe. He is the 'first fruits', the 'pioneer of life'. He has forced open a door that has been locked since the death of the first man. He has met, fought, and beaten the King of Death. Everything is different because He has done so. This is the beginning of the New Creation: a new chapter in cosmic history has opened.[7]

The genius of God's gospel mission is that it subverted all expectations, *including* the devil's. The devil is thwarted because he simply doesn't know what he wants. One minute he is deflecting Jesus from the cross; the next he is propelling him there. His tactics depend on a combination of deception, betrayal and force. He exploits worldly powers and strategies (such as the Roman emperor and his provincial governors) who have always thrown their weight around, oppressing the people and crushing opposition. So what does God do? He sends a King unlike any other. He will suffer, he will be humiliated, and he will be defeated. Which is precisely how he will be victorious. Like a martial arts black belt, Jesus redirects

---

7 C. S. Lewis, *Miracles: A preliminary study* (London: HarperCollins, 2002), pp. 236–7.

the full force of the devil's attack back on his assailant. His weakness became the very means for defeating Satan.

Death could not keep its hold on him.

Jesus has won. Jesus is alive.

Questions to consider

1 How might you explain the significance of Jesus' resurrection to a sceptic?
2 What happens to the gospel if Jesus' resurrection is only spiritual or metaphorical?

6

Spirit life: the Christian life made possible

A single moment can determine the direction of an entire life.

Mark Hamill was a young actor with small roles in soap operas and sitcoms. A friend of his, Robert Englund, was auditioning for a new science fiction movie but thought Hamill would be a far better fit than him, so suggested his name. Hamill then auditioned for the part in *Star Wars* and got it, and became inescapably and permanently identified with Luke Skywalker. The drawback was that he was unable to get cast in other films until he reprised Skywalker years later. Still, he is philosophical about it and grateful for the astonishing opportunities the role brought him.

Tommie Smith and John Carlos were African American sprinters who won the 200m gold and bronze medals, respectively, at the 1968 Mexico Olympics. They decided to use the medal ceremony as an opportunity to make a civil rights protest, with the collaboration of the white Australian silver medallist, Peter Norman. Smith and Carlos were shoeless, but wore black socks, raising their black-gloved hands in the Black power salute with their heads bowed. The photograph of the ceremony ended up on the next day's front pages all over the world. All three faced vitriolic criticism and ostracism. None regretted their actions, but none would ever represent their countries again.

Then there was the fellow-student from my time at university – let's call her 'Alison'. Alison was one of those people who was a joy to have around, guaranteed to bring a smile when it was most needed. She was happy-go-lucky, keen to live life to its fullest, keen to try anything. It was perhaps inevitable that she would try marijuana and, at first, she was fine, enjoying the sensation of lightness and calm. But within a few days, out of the blue, she became psychotic and had to be hospitalised. Despite trying it only once, the medical consensus was that the marijuana had caused her illness. Initially planning to take a year out from her course, she ended up dropping out altogether.

Three contrasting, life-changing moments: one serendipitous, one courageous, one tragic. These may be hard to relate to. For most of us, life continues uneventfully and predictably. But the reality is that there *is* a moment that is available to each one of us – one that does not simply determine the rest of our lives, but our eternity. To see this, we now turn to John's Gospel where we see something of the transformation that comes when people encounter Jesus.

Born to new life

As we have seen, the Old Testament anticipated an extraordinary afterlife for the Messiah. But it also foresaw that what was true for him might also be true for those who follow him. It is fascinating then that the disciples' dawning understanding accompanied the first glimmers of hope. John's Gospel is perhaps the Gospel that ties this hope of life most closely to Jesus' mission. Before this early conversation takes place, Jesus has performed his most startling miracles to date. He provided lunch for a vast crowd with the meagre ingredients of some bread and a couple of fish (John 6:1–15). (It is often overlooked that all four Gospels merely inform us that five thousand men were present, so perhaps there were also as many women and children again.) Then, more privately, he walks on the surface of Lake Galilee, out to the disciples in their fishing boat. Their initial terror quickly becomes astonishment as they help him clamber aboard (John 6:16–24). Wowed by the feeding miracle, the crowds are understandably keen for more spectacles and so they chase him to the eastern side of the lake. This is hardly the ideal motivation and Jesus knows it, so he raises the bar. He effectively tells them that they should come to him not because of what they can get out of him but because of who he is: he is 'the bread of life' (John 6:35). This comes after he has explained the correct response of followers. 'The work of God is this: to believe in the one he has sent' (John 6:29).

This is too much for many. They are put off by his demands, perhaps because Jesus appears to be so self-focused. It is astonishing how much he talks about *himself*. On anybody else's lips, much of his teaching would be the ravings of a deranged egomaniac. Even a cursory reading of the Gospels shows that this assessment could not be less accurate when it comes to Jesus. He is always measured and calm, sensitive and generous, constantly keeping an eye out for the vulnerable or ostracised. We are eventually forced to draw the same conclusion as the disciples: he is teaching these things because they are true, and we need them. It is not because he has a hyper-inflated ego. This is what makes this small interaction between Jesus and his disciples so significant.

> From this time many of his disciples turned back and no longer followed him.
>
> 'You do not want to leave too, do you?' Jesus asked the Twelve.
>
> Simon Peter answered him, 'Lord, to whom shall we go? You have the words of eternal life. We have come to believe and to know that you are the Holy One of God.'
> (John 6:66–9)

Peter says they are not going anywhere. Jesus is the key to real living, the gateway to eternal life. That is why the disciples have come to trust him. As Jesus has already said, 'Very truly I tell you, the one who believes has eternal life. I am the bread of life' (John 6:47–8). In other words, eternal life has begun. It starts at the very moment that someone first puts their trust in him. It is a revolutionary moment.

Of course, the transformation this trust brings is so all-encompassing that nobody can bring it about themselves. Early on, Jesus is approached after dark by a senior religious leader, Nicodemus, evidently anxious to keep their meeting under wraps. He comes presumably because of his confused fascination with the question: just who is this man? God is clearly at work through Jesus, but Jesus fits none of the categories people had for someone sent from heaven. Jesus won't be diverted by speculation, however sincere. Instead, he makes a bald statement of spiritual reality: 'Very truly I tell you, no one can see the kingdom of God unless they are born again' (John 3:3). Nicodemus is very confused, taking Jesus literally. In response, he merely gets the same point expanded, if somewhat enigmatically.

> Jesus answered, 'Very truly I tell you, no one can enter the kingdom of God unless they are born of water and the Spirit. Flesh gives birth to flesh, but the Spirit gives birth to spirit. You should not be surprised at my saying, "You must be born again." The wind blows wherever it pleases. You hear its sound, but you cannot tell where it comes from or where it is going. So it is with everyone born of the Spirit.'
> (John 3:5–8)

Our overfamiliarity with the phrase, even in today's secular-ised popular culture – 'Oh, you're not one of those *born-again* Christians, are you?' – masks its weirdness. No wonder Nicodemus is confused. Even if we grasp that it cannot be literal, it is hard to know what Jesus is driving at. His central contrast is between the physical and the spiritual, but in both cases, birth is not an act of the one born. 'Flesh gives birth to flesh': my life began at conception in my mother's womb. I had nothing to do with it. So it is with new spiritual life, what Jesus calls the rebirth. Only God's Holy Spirit brings that about. I cannot claim the slightest credit for my own rebirth. The fact that he operates invisibly is no reason to be sceptical, which is why he is like the wind. On the morning after a hurricane, only a fool would dispute the wind's existence or potency. What's more, despite the educated guesses of meteorolo-gists, it is hard to predict exactly where the wind will go next. It is the same with the Spirit. We cannot control or manipulate him. But look at his accomplishments. He can enable someone to be born again. There is an echo here of the prophet Ezekiel's vision of the valley filled with an army's bones (Ezekiel 37). Could those bones live? Only God knows. Can a person be born again? Only God knows. Only God can pull it off.

But surely, if only God can do this, human beings are left without agency or responsibility? Not necessarily. Imagine a friend has a serious tumour for which the only known cure is several hours under the surgeon's knife. She faces a choice. Will she go into hospital or not? Both options carry their risks. She must weigh them up to figure out which gives the better chance of survival. To opt for the operation, she is to place herself completely at the surgeon's mercy; if not, she is at the mercy of the disease. If she chooses the former and it is successful, she can take no credit. Only the medical team have that right. She will spend the entire time unconscious! The only thing that does depend on her is the initial decision.

Jesus offers his new 'birth', the way to eternal life for those who trust him. There is no obligation to do so. After all, some of Jesus' followers leave him in John 6. The decision to put trust in him is the equivalent of walking into the hospital and prepping for surgery. Calling on readers to do this is precisely why John writes his Gospel. Notice how he summarises his purpose towards the book's conclusion:

> Jesus performed many other signs in the presence of his disciples, which are not recorded in this book. But these are written that you may *believe* that Jesus is the Messiah, the Son of God, and that by *believing* you may have life in his name. (John 20:30–1, my emphasis)

This is a declaration of Jesus' identity, in all its beautiful complexity, with the explicit goal of readers trusting in him. That is the route to overcoming death. That is the way of eternal life. All because of Jesus' own victory. He is our great champion who conquers death on our behalf, just like that unprepossessing teenager David up against the Philistine giant, Goliath (1 Samuel 17). That is just as well, since none of us has the slightest hope in defeating death. As we have seen repeatedly, our mortality is inescapable. This is why the resurrection (and not just the cross) features so prominently in John's Gospel, and, for that matter, in the rest of the New

Testament. Jesus is propelled by his mission towards his glory. It is shocking that his execution might be a manifestation of that glory, but it does not come in isolation. As D. A. Carson comments after Jesus' miraculous provision of wine at the Cana wedding:

> His glory would be revealed in greatest measure in his cross, resurrection and exaltation, but every step along the course of his ministry was an adumbration of that glory. The glory was not visible to all who had seen the miracle; the glory cannot be identified with the miraculous display.[1]

We get a sense of that in Table 2, which outlines several places in John's Gospel where the correspondence between trusting in Jesus' identity and the life that he brings is made most explicitly.

Jesus is not preaching some kind of afterlife message that makes little difference to this life. In his mind, eternal life has *already* begun, at the very moment a person first believes in him (equivalent to going into hospital for that operation). It is also important to understand that Jesus' insistence on the need for being born again is entirely consistent with other New Testament writers.

- John picks up on the idea in his first letter: 'Everyone who believes that Jesus is the Christ is born of God, and everyone who loves the father loves his child as well' (1 John 5:1).
- Peter's logic is similar to John's. In this life, we experience a second birth and a living hope (we might translate that as 'an active' hope), all because of Jesus' victory: 'Praise be to the God and Father of our Lord Jesus Christ! In his great mercy he has given us new birth into a living hope through the resurrection of Jesus Christ from the dead' (1 Peter 1:3).
- James shows how this new life comes about when God speaks it into existence, a key stage in his renewal of the whole of creation: 'He chose to give us birth through the word of truth, that we might be a kind of firstfruits of all he created' (James 1:18).

---

1   D. A. Carson, *The Gospel According to John* (Leicester: IVP, 1991), p. 175.

Table 2 The result of trusting Jesus in John's Gospel

	Cause or sign	Object	Response	Result
John 3:14–16	As Moses lifted snake... so Son of Man must be lifted	Son of Man, One and only Son	Believe	Will not perish but have eternal life
John 3:35–6	Father loves Son, placed everything in his hands	The Son	Believe	Has eternal life
John 5:24	Whoever hears my word	Him who has sent me	Believe	Has eternal life, will not be judged but has crossed over from death to life
John 6:35	Feeding of 5,000	I am the bread of life	Come to me, believe in me	Never go hungry... never be thirsty
John 6:40	The Father's will	The Son	Look to him, believe in him	Shall have eternal life, I will raise up on last day
John 11:25–6	Lazarus resuscitated	I am the resurrection and the life	Believe in me	Will live, even though dies... will never die
John 14:5–6	Thomas: Where are you going?	I am the Way, Truth, Life	Come through me	Come to the Father
John 20:30–1	These signs are written	Jesus is the Messiah, Son of God	Believe	Have life in his name

- When Paul writes to Titus, he is emphatic about our dependence on God's grace for this new life: 'he saved us, not because of righteous things we had done, but because of his mercy. He saved us through the washing of rebirth and renewal by the Holy Spirit' (Titus 3:5).
- Finally, Paul also describes the start of the Christian life in terms that are, if anything, even more eye-popping. It is like the creation of the world, again brought about by Christ: 'Therefore,

if anyone is in Christ, the new creation has come: the old has gone, the new is here! All this is from God, who reconciled us to himself through Christ' (2 Corinthians 5:17–18).

This is authentic, first-century Christianity. Each of us needs to be born again into eternal life.

Empowered for new life

Return briefly with me to the operation to remove the tumour. The surgery was successful, and the doctors are very pleased with the results. However, it will take time to adjust to the new reality. The good news is that the symptoms which alerted the doctors to the tumour's presence in the first place have gone. Our friend's speech is no longer slurred and she no longer has trouble with hand–eye coordination. But she finds she has to change some aspects of her lifestyle. She can't simply turn the clock back to the carefree days of her youth. She must be careful after the surgical pummelling her body has endured. Still, it saved her life.

A Christian new birth obviously does not cause the trauma of a major operation, but it does have repercussions and consequences. It transforms our attitudes, our priorities, our lifestyles. We will come on to what that looks like. For now, we need to grasp *how* that happens. The Apostle Paul grappled with that question deeply and tackles the subject in several letters. Here, he ties this new life explicitly to Jesus' resurrection: 'And if the Spirit of him who raised Jesus from the dead is living in you, he who raised Christ from the dead will also give life to your mortal bodies because of his Spirit who lives in you' (Romans 8:11).

The logic is simple. Jesus was dead. The Holy Spirit brought him back to life. If we trust in our champion Christ, the same Spirit comes to live within us. What he did for Jesus, he will do for us. Notice that Paul insists that our bodies are still mortal. Despite what some preachers might claim, coming to Christ does not result in the kind of immortality that prevents us from ever getting sick or dying. The resurrection in view here is the one that will happen in the future, *after* our deaths. This will be our life in Christ that comes after death,

Table 3 The three stages of resurrection

Resurrection tense	Our experience	In God's family
Past resurrection: Our conversion	Regeneration, or second birth	We are reborn into God's new family
Present resurrection: Our conflict	Mortification, or crucifying the sinful nature	We increasingly take on the family likeness
Future resurrection: Our conviction	Perfection, or complete 'Christlikeness'	We are united with the whole family of God

our life after life. But Paul's equivalent to eternal life already having started for the believer comes in this verse in what the Spirit is doing now. He 'lives in you'. He is at work in us, transforming us, making us more like the Christ who died and rose for us, as Table 3 shows. It seeks to make what we can call the 'tenses of resurrection' clear.[2] The Spirit makes all this possible because he is with us.

Another lens through which to make sense of what it means to enjoy Christ's resurrection for ourselves is the wonder of our being united with Jesus. This lies at the heart of Paul's argument in Romans 6, where he uses a person's baptism to represent their rebirth at conversion. The symbolism of going under the water and then re-emerging from it at baptism points us to Christ going into the tomb and breaking out of death's chains. This is why he can say we are 'therefore buried with him through baptism into death in order that, just as Christ was raised from the dead through the glory of the Father, we too may live a new life' (Romans 6:4). What makes this possible is that we are forever bound to him.

> For if we have been united with him in a death like his, we will certainly also be united with him in a resurrection like his… Now if we died with Christ, we believe that we will also live with him. For we know that since Christ was raised from the dead, he cannot die again; death no longer has mastery over him. (Romans 6:5, 8–9)

---

2 Further explanations of this table may be found in chapter 11 of Meynell, *Cross-Examined*, revised and expanded ed. (London: IVP, 2021).

Because of Jesus, then, we will die but live again. Where he went, we will go.

This puts us in his debt. He did all this for us. We owe him everything. We cannot possibly repay it, of course, since his gift of grace is priceless. But it does mean we now have an obligation.

> In the same way, count yourselves dead to sin but alive to God in Christ Jesus. Therefore do not let sin reign in your mortal body so that you obey its evil desires.
> (Romans 6:11–12)

Again, this does not mean we become sinless at conversion, no more than we become immune to mortality. It means that we live in between two realities simultaneously. We have been raised with Christ, and we live by his Spirit. This gives us the mind-boggling hope of being with him for eternity after our deaths. While we wait for that fulfilment, we are still mortal, broken and fallen. We ought not let 'sin reign in [our] mortal body'. But we are not helpless or hopeless. We have God's Spirit living within us. He is the guarantor of our hope.

When we lived in central London, I would often walk past a plaque on a house built on the site where the great pioneering scientist Michael Faraday first worked as a laboratory apprentice. His brilliant mind ranged over all kinds of different scientific fields, although he is best known for his work on electromagnetism. He was so significant that he was commemorated in the 1990s on the £20 note and Albert Einstein hung his portrait in his study. The renowned British physicist Ernest Rutherford said of him:

> When we consider the magnitude and extent of his discoveries and their influence on the progress of science and of industry, there is no honour too great to pay to the memory of Faraday, one of the greatest scientific discoverers of all time.[3]

---

3 J. M. Thomas, *Michael Faraday and the Royal Institution* (Bristol: Hilger, 1991), p. 129.

Less well known is the fact that Faraday was a man of deep Christian convictions, which he regarded as integral to his scientific research. Towards the end of his life, the story is told of some journalists who asked him to speculate about life after death.

> Speculations! I know nothing about speculations. I'm resting on certainties. I know that my Redeemer liveth and because he lives, I shall live also.

He was a man who knew what being bound to Christ in his death and resurrection meant.

Questions to consider

1 How would you reply to a friend who says, 'Oh, I believe in Jesus but I'm not one of those *born-again* Christians?'
2 What is the significance of Jesus' miracles (or as John calls them in his Gospel, 'signs') for believers today? What resulting obligations do believers now have?

7

Life signs: the Christian life energised

We do not hear from the so-called New Atheists as much as we did twenty years ago. Perhaps their ideas were too radical and disturbing for modern people. After all, few people enjoy being told that their lives are cosmically meaningless. As Richard Dawkins famously put it:

> In a universe of electrons and selfish genes, blind physical forces and genetic replication, some people are going to get hurt, other people are going to get lucky, and you won't find any rhyme or reason in it, nor any justice. The universe that we observe has precisely the properties we should expect if there is, at bottom, no design, no purpose, no evil, no good, nothing but pitiless indifference. DNA neither knows nor cares. DNA just is, and we dance to its music.[1]

That is quite the statement. Yet, credit where credit is due, he sticks by it. It is one reason Dawkins has given public backing to a youth organisation that for the last twenty-five years has run humanist summer camps for children from secular, 'free-thinking' homes. They exist to help them have fun while engaging with 'astronomy, critical thinking, philosophy and pseudo-science'. One highlight of the camps is apparently 'Hunt the Unicorn'. The kids are told that the campsite is in fact home to two unicorns despite being invisible and undetectable by sound, smell or trace. They are then informed

---

1 Richard Dawkins, *River out of Eden: A Darwinian view of life* (London: Phoenix, 1996), p. 133.

that every single leader believes in these unicorns because of a 'book that has been handed down through the ages' but which is 'too precious for anyone to see'.[2] Any child who can successfully prove the non-existence of unicorns gets a prize: either a £10 note with Charles Darwin's image on it signed by Richard Dawkins himself, or if in the US, a so-called 'godless' $100 bill printed before 1957 when the phrase 'In God We Trust' was added.

The point is hardly subtle. Fascinating conversations are provoked, I'm sure, but the agenda is clear. Belief in God and the Bible is as irrational as belief in invisible unicorns and their mysterious ancient, unread book. It is all imaginary – which is to say, made-up nonsense. For many, something may not be counted as true or important until it can be tested in laboratory conditions or proven mathematically. That is a kind of proper, 'grown-up' truth. But if it cannot be sensed (by sound, sight, taste, feel or smell), we presume it cannot be real. This has been the accumulated legacy of four centuries of Western philosophy and culture.

The flaw is that it is far too simplistic. As well as deceptive. All kinds of things defy its logic. Just take the idea of beauty. It is notoriously hard to define or prove. But few deny beauty is real. Or how about love? What is love, exactly? I don't mean romantic feelings here. They float in and out but rarely last (which is why relationships exclusively grounded on romance are so tragically brief). I mean love as the ideal of sacrificial giving to another. Some scientific explanations of love get offered – such as some kind of deep, evolutionary impulse to preserve the species or something. But they reduce everything too far, robbing love of its wonder and mysterious power. Does that mean we must conclude such love is meaningless or impossible? Surely not? Of course, the New Atheists' concern is not with abstract concepts but gods, and especially the Christian God (they tend to be more reticent about other deities). They insist that God is imaginary, Jesus only human (if

---

2 Steven Morris, 'The Great Unicorn Hunt', *The Guardian*, 29 July 2009, https://www.the-guardian.com/science/2009/jul/29/camp-quest-richard-dawkins, (accessed 25 July 2023). Courtesy of Guardian News & Media Ltd.

they concede his existence, that is), and the Bible of historical and cultural value at best but pernicious fairy tales at worst.

The contention of this book is that God *has* intervened in human history, culminating in Jesus' life, death and resurrection. The Bible does not consist in fabrication but testimony, written by those who witnessed or experienced divine revelation and activity. That is what makes it true. Yet, some will feel unsettled by what I say next.

We often need to *imagine* some aspects of the Christian life to be true of us.

Doesn't that put us squarely in the New Atheists' crosshairs? We can almost hear them. 'There you go! See! It's all made up. They have to imagine it to believe it. It's just like unicorns!' But the fact that something needs to be imagined – perhaps because it is invisible to the naked eye, or inaudible, or beyond our understanding – does not mean it is unreal or fake. It is simply taken on trust. The writer to the Hebrews defined Christian faith as 'confidence in what we hope for and assurance about what we do not see' (Hebrews 11:1). In other words, it is a matter of trusting in future outcomes and invisible realities. That is, of course, hard to do. New Atheists insist it is absurd. But there is one excellent reason for believing something that is difficult or impossible to prove to a sceptic: we trust the one who told us to believe it. Given what we have been considering about Jesus, it should be clear why so many do trust him. He rose from the dead!

God made us with imaginations. All of us. This is far more essential than we might realise. Too often it gets associated with so-called 'creatives' because they earn a living from what they dream up. Playwrights, novelists, composers, artists: they are supposedly different from mere mortals because they have special gifts. For example, I'm always astonished by the ability of an architect to see a patch of waste ground and draw up plans that would entirely transform the experience of being in that place. That takes real imagination. But it is not just 'creatives'. Scientists could never dream up new theories to explain their observations without imagination. Engineers and logistics managers need it to figure out solutions to complex problems. But why restrict it? The simple demands of everyday life depend on frequent use of the imagination. We couldn't plan our diaries without imagining scenarios or clashes. We couldn't go to the supermarket without imagining the meals we will make. And we need our imaginations to thrive in the Christian life. The world around us constantly throws up alternative, competing ways of understanding life. They are often compelling and attractive; they wouldn't have many takers otherwise. It often requires an act of Christian imagination to resist these and to see how much better it is to base our lives on a far stronger, deeper narrative, one whose bedrock is God's plan to redeem his creation. It is not a question of gritting our teeth and tensing every sinew in order to try to believe something false. We use our imaginations to see how something unseen or anticipated might apply to us. That helps us to live in the present as if what is to come has already begun, despite appearances to the contrary.

God's living buildings

Peter was not the only apostle who liked to mix his metaphors. Paul was fond of doing it too. A good example comes from his first Corinthian letter, but it only works if we engage our imaginations. He needs us to trust in a reality that seems to be contradicted by what we actually see. That is why many perhaps miss how startling it is. When people hear the word 'church' today, they most likely think of a building, perhaps especially an old one, and, more often than not, one that is locked up and empty. That could not be further from the New Testament meaning of the word it translates (*ekklesia*), since it originally had nothing to do with buildings and everything to do with a gathering of people. That is what makes Paul's idea so odd. 'Don't you know that you yourselves are God's temple and that God's Spirit lives among you?' (1 Corinthians 3:16).

In context, Paul is explaining that even though different people have been involved in the founding and nurturing of God's church in Corinth, the only one who can legitimately take credit for its existence is God himself. Only God can 'make things grow' (1 Corinthians 3:7). This is why Paul can describe his team as 'fellow workers in God's service; you are God's field, God's building' (1

Corinthians 3:9). I doubt this second analogy would even have occurred to ordinary believers without Paul's prompting. Even when a crowd gathers, most would reach for other descriptions before using an architectural one. Of course, even though the ancient world was strewn with temples, he has only one in mind: the Jewish Temple at the centre of Jerusalem. Suggesting the rag-tag bunch of Corinthian Christians had even the remotest connection with that holy place would have struck most devout people as bordering on the sacrilegious. It entails quite the imaginative leap.

A few pages on in the same letter, Paul stretches the metaphor even further. Now, it refers not simply to the body of believers, but individual church members.

> Do you not know that your bodies are temples of the Holy Spirit, who is in you, whom you have received from God? You are not your own; you were bought at a price. Therefore honour God with your bodies.
> (1 Corinthians 6:19–20)

Paul was spurred to write this by disturbing news of relationship breakdown, cheating and lawsuits between church members. As so often in his New Testament correspondence, his argument is simple: 'Be who you are! You are so valuable that God in Christ considered the cross to be a price worth paying. You belong to him. So, behave like it!' But his temple analogy gives his point greater weight here as we will see.

One of the Bible's most consistent themes, a thread running from Genesis to Revelation, is that of Immanuel, 'God with us'. At the very beginning, we see God with the man and woman in the Garden of Eden (Genesis 2); and at the end his 'dwelling-place is now among the people, and he will dwell with them' (Revelation 21:3). The entire, intervening story can be seen as the divine reversal of the devastation of the Fall (Genesis 3), designed in part to restore that proximity and intimacy. When the people were gathered at Mount Sinai after the Exodus, God gave detailed instructions for managing this proximity until the time of sin's final eradication.[3] In the old covenant, he would dwell in the heart of the Israelite camp symbolically, in a tent of his own known as the Tabernacle (Exodus 26). This was the blueprint for the Temple built under King Solomon and rebuilt by King Herod the Great around Jesus' birth. It was unmissable to any Jerusalem visitor, easily one of the most visible buildings in the region and of profound significance for Jewish believers. For this is where God dwelt with his people, albeit behind heavy barriers. They were never designed to pen God in (as if that were possible) but to protect sinful people from God's holiness. There was access to God, but it was curtailed in considerable ways and only possible after various rituals and sacrifices.

By the time we reach the New Testament, God's purpose for this Temple has been fulfilled. The letter to the Hebrews in particular views it as a temporary measure, since, for one thing, it is 'impossible for the blood of bulls and goats to take away sins' (Hebrews 10:4). Once Christ has died and risen, the physical Temple is redundant. In fact, Jesus is simultaneously the Great High Priest and supreme sacrifice for sin, a sacrifice not offered in the physical Temple but in the court of heaven itself (Hebrews 9:23–4). That is far superior to anything on earth. As we have already seen, he is the embodiment of what the Temple was always meant to point to: the place to meet God.

When Paul describes the Corinthian Christians, both corporately and individually, as temples of God's Spirit, he is simply drawing out more implications of being united to Christ. If Jesus is God's Temple and we belong to him, then so are we. If God is living within us, then it is entirely legitimate to say that each of us can be a place for someone to meet God. This is central to our witness to the world. But we barely live up to such a high calling which is why our witness is so impoverished. We resemble any other social grouping in the world, apparently subject to all the dynamics, tensions and challenges we might expect anywhere. The idea that we might be

---

3 Not coincidentally, the ancient Greek translation of Deuteronomy 4:10 uses the word *ekklesia* for the gathering of the people at the base of Mount Sinai, or Mount Horeb as it is called there.

God's temple despite our flaws and fights is a stretch of the imagination, to say the least. But imagination is precisely what it requires when the evidence before us seems lacking. For God in Christ has achieved this. And he lives within us by his Spirit. Despite appearances, we are not human units, scattered and isolated, but people rescued at great cost to be bound to Christ and one another. We are living buildings. Temples. Each of us, together *and* apart. We are a means by which a lost and confused world might be found by God. We will only take that responsibility seriously if we fire up our imaginations to do justice to what it means to live out Paul's metaphor. But we are so much more than God's temples.

God's living letters

It is undoubtedly standard practice and probably impossible to prevent, despite the ethical grey areas. Potential employers are no longer forced to rely on applicants' covering letters, CVs and references. The inescapability of social media means that only a tiny minority will have failed to leave some kind of discoverable digital footprint. The modern world overwhelms us with the ease in which we can dig up information about strangers almost anywhere in the world. Past indiscretions, views now regarded as unpalatable, let alone supposedly private activity – all this and more is accessible to even the casual surfer. How different life was even just a generation ago, let alone in the ancient world; but people managed somehow. Especially for those who travelled around the Roman Empire, as many of the apostles did, letters of introduction were essential.

If there was a church that caused Paul and his colleagues more heartache and tears than any other, it was surely that of Corinth. Not only did several moral challenges threaten the fellowship, but some members had concluded that Paul's influence itself was central to the church's problems. This was acutely painful. It is impossible not to take disputes personally when they are directed personally. Still, Paul perseveres with them with surprising patience and generosity. Despite the seriousness of the problems, he insists on calling them brothers and sisters (2 Corinthians 1:8, 8:1, 13:11). He appeals to their shared history, their friendships over several years. This, to Paul's mind, is the best antidote to the poison spread about him.

> You yourselves are our letter, written on our hearts, known and read by everyone. You show that you are a letter from Christ, the result of our ministry, written not with ink but with the Spirit of the living God, not on tablets of stone but on tablets of human hearts.
> (2 Corinthians 3:2–3)

Opponents perhaps disparaged Paul's ministry as inferior because he is too lax about some ethical matters, too ready to compromise over the cultural markers of Jewish identity and society. They are also faintly embarrassed by his apparently unsophisticated speaking styles or method, especially when it comes to public debates with Corinth's movers and shakers. But they are being forgetful. For how did the church come to exist in Corinth in the first place? It was through the ministry of Paul, Apollos and others (1 Corinthians 3:5–9). He is not boasting but simply stating what happened. He knows that only God can take the credit. As we have seen already, Paul is merely a worker in God's service, while the church that has been planted and built, belongs exclusively to God (1 Corinthians 3:9). Thus, the very existence of the Corinthian church is clear evidence of God's work in this brash, chaotic, double-port city. They themselves are Paul's letter of introduction, they are all the validation he needs. The 'Spirit of the living God' has written this endorsement letter on their hearts, unlike normal human correspondence. Notice Paul mixing his metaphors yet again, merging the imagery of the endorsement letter with the old covenant law revealed to Moses on Mount Sinai. But there is more to it even than that. The prophets eagerly anticipated the day when every one of God's covenant people would be given the means by which to keep, as well as know, God's law.

> I will give you a new heart and put a new spirit in you; I will remove from you your heart of stone and give you a heart of

flesh. And I will put my Spirit in you and move you to follow
my decrees and be careful to keep my laws.
(Ezekiel 36:26–7)

So, it is the God-promised, Spirit-led heart-transplant in each
believer which results in this evidence, the signs of a new life.

I love listening to people sharing how they came to faith. It is
so encouraging as well as fascinating to grasp the huge variety in
how God works in people. I was speaking recently at a summer
family camp for a church in western Turkey. They have been
meeting at the same venue for twenty-five years and a highlight
is always the baptisms on the Saturday morning. They set the
whole morning aside for it, giving each candidate the chance to
share something of their stories. This year, there were thirteen.
All but one were from Muslim backgrounds (of varying degrees
of previous commitment), all have paid considerable costs in
making such a bold and public statement. Perhaps because I was
thinking about writing this chapter as I listened, it was striking to
hear of several being set on the road to Christ when they noticed
the changed lifestyles of other friends who had converted. One or
two were in difficult marriages; one or two had felt imprisoned by
deep mental pain and anxiety; one or two were facing intolerable
challenges at work and despaired about matters improving. In
their accounts, they shared how they noticed such big differences
in new believers that it stopped them in their tracks. They were
forced to acknowledge that *something* was happening, however it
might be explained.

This is what Paul is getting at with the Corinthians. After all,
it is nothing short of miraculous that there was a church there at
all. The city was insecurely self-conscious of its own importance
as a Roman provincial capital and trading hub since its historical
pedigree couldn't quite match Athens down the road. As a port city
(with a harbour on either side of the Corinthian isthmus on the
Adriatic and Aegean seas), it was notoriously rough and intimidating. It must have felt like the last place on earth where citizens
might turn their backs on its religious and cultural inheritance. But

there *was* a church there. If there can be a church in Corinth, there can be a church anywhere. They were letters sent from the living Christ himself, evidence that he was active even here.

While receiving a personal letter from him would be a thrill, it is clear that a person can communicate so much more than words on a page ever could. No life can be reduced to sentences and paragraphs, powerful and affecting though they can be. A person is so much more. That is why the changes brought about by God's new life can make such an impact. God's work is ongoing, a process that lasts a lifetime. But this process can feel very confusing at times, for at least two reasons.

It can feel like we're declining morally

A friend once likened the Holy Spirit's process of change in a person's life to living near a large, derelict house which had just been bought. A young couple were trying to do as much of the work on it themselves, so it was inevitably taking an age. But for locals, they could see incremental change, as piece by piece, elements were painstakingly repaired, replaced or improved. Jesus tells us that when he returns to his Father, he will send his Spirit to 'prove the world to be in the wrong about sin and righteousness and judgment' (John 16:8). But he also casts his gaze on the Church. We are convicted of our own failings, necessary even decades after coming to Christ.

That can be hard, simply because there is always *something* to face. Because that is a constant in this life, we can feel as if we are never making progress at all. Or worse. As sins that have been long hidden or dormant are brought into the light, it might seem as if we are going backwards. In my experience with older believers, however, the godlier they seem to others, the more sinful they seem to themselves. It is simply that God has his timing for working through these darker recesses of the human heart. But when that is happening, a person's witness is all the more potent. We really are God's living letters, even when we feel like failures. As one preacher used to quip, Christians are like a church spire: the closer they get to God, the smaller they become.

It can feel like we're declining physically

It seems perfectly logical at first, which is why so many are taken in by it. But if we have God's Spirit living within us, the same Spirit who raised Jesus from the dead, surely we should become immune to the sufferings and sicknesses of the world? It is quite a thought, and one that is certainly attractive, especially if offered to someone in agony. The problem is that it is palpably a lie. For a start, everybody dies, as we have seen. And nobody really dies of 'old age'; they die of an increasingly complex convergence of diseases and afflictions. God can and clearly does heal some people at particular moments. But, in the end, nobody is healed permanently. We all die. Our lives propel us towards that inevitability.

This brings us to the final life-sign to exercise our imagination muscle.

God's living ambassadors

To look at any human being is to see someone finite, mortal. We are limited in almost every conceivable way. And gradually, different parts of our bodies begin to fail. The temptation is to think that just as our bodies decline, so will God's work in us. It feels like a contradiction, as if it might somehow undermine the spiritual work God is accomplishing within us. But Paul is insistent:

> Though outwardly we are wasting away, yet inwardly we are being renewed day by day. For our light and momentary troubles are achieving for us an eternal glory that far outweighs them all. So we fix our eyes not on what is seen, but on what is unseen, since what is seen is temporary, but what is unseen is eternal.
> (2 Corinthians 4:16–18)

Perhaps you have visited an older member of your church fellowship in hospital, and you are shocked to see someone you knew as vital and energetic lying prone and surrounded by tubes, monitors and bleeps. There seems nothing at all glorious about this scene.

But this is where we need an act of the imagination. We take on trust what is *really* going on here.

One of the most famous sermons that C. S. Lewis ever preached was given in the University Church of St Mary's, in Oxford, in June 1941. The Second World War had no obvious end in sight: Britain was alone in Europe; just a couple of weeks later, Hitler ripped up the Nazi–Soviet pact by marching on Moscow; Japan's attack on Pearl Harbour would drag the United States into the war only four months later. This was a dark time in Britain, such that many must have felt resigned to grim futures. If ever there was a time when everything felt as if it was going wrong, this was it. But Lewis was determined to help his listeners see beyond the superficial and immediate to a deeper, eternal reality. He wants us to embrace the implications of the eternal glory that Paul said belonged to all believers. As Lewis put it, we must sense the 'weight of glory'.[4] This is how he draws the sermon to a close:

> It may be possible for each to think too much of his own potential glory hereafter; it is hardly possible for him to think too often or too deeply about that of his neighbour. The load, or weight, or burden of my neighbour's glory should be laid on my back, a load so heavy that only humility can carry it, and the backs of the proud will be broken. It is a serious thing to live in a society of possible gods and goddesses, to remember that the dullest and most uninteresting person you can talk to may one day be a creature which, if you saw it now, you would be strongly tempted to worship, or else a horror and a corruption such as you now meet, if at all, only in a nightmare.

At this point, Lewis appeals to our imaginations so that we ignore the temporary appearance of things.

---

4 C. S. Lewis, *The Weight of Glory, and Other Addresses* (New York, NY: HarperOne, 2001), chapter 1.

There are no *ordinary* people. You have never talked to a mere mortal. Nations, cultures, arts, civilisations – these are mortal, and their life is to ours as the life of a gnat. But it is immortals whom we joke with, work with, marry, snub, and exploit – immortal horrors or everlasting splendours. This does not mean that we are to be perpetually solemn. We must play. But our merriment must be of that kind (and it is, in fact, the merriest kind) which exists between people who have, from the outset, taken each other seriously – no flippancy, no superiority, no presumption... your neighbour is the holiest object presented to your senses.[5]

Because Christ's Spirit lives within us, Lewis is saying, we can now be described as *immortals*. We belong elsewhere; that is where our allegiance lies. But we work here; this is where our duties lie. This explains why Paul will go on to describe his ministry in diplomatic terms.

We are therefore Christ's ambassadors, as though God were making his appeal through us. We implore you on Christ's behalf: be reconciled to God. God made him who had no sin to be sin for us, so that in him we might become the right-eousness of God.
(2 Corinthians 5:20–1)

God has made us alive in Christ by his Spirit. We belong to one another as we belong to him. We are his building. We have been transformed by God's Spirit, and as such are living testimonies to the people around us. We are living letters of recommenda-tion from and about the one who saved us. We have been given sight of eternal realities, which must be imagined to be believed. But they are realities, nonetheless. We are visible despite wasting away, we are earthly despite our heavenly citizenship. We are thus Christ's ambassadors representing and declaring his purposes to

---

5 Lewis, *The Weight of Glory, and Other Addresses*, pp. 45–6.

a world that doesn't know him. We present an alternative way of inhabiting the world though the way we live, one that resists the dehumanising or despairing narratives swirling around us. This is why Peter, for one, counsels his readers always to 'be prepared to give an answer to everyone who asks you to give a reason for the hope' that we have (1 Peter 3:15).

All this is possible now for one simple reason: we are truly alive.

Questions to consider

1 Why is the imagination important for our discipleship? How is this different from believing something we know to be false?
2 Believers are described as living buildings, letters and ambassadors. Consider how each image might make a difference to how you go about the coming week.

Part 3

FUTURE: TRUE LIFE REVEALED

Isn't the idea of life after life an impossible fantasy, something unimaginable and unreal? It is certainly hard to conceive of what it might actually be *like*. But this is why the Apostle John's vision of eternity recorded in the book of Revelation is so important. This is the heart of Christian hope, and it spurs us on to live in the present *for* our King in confident expectation of a future *with* our King. While John never provides us with exhaustive details, we are given enough to rest a living confidence in our returning king.

8

Immanuel: practising
the presence

There is a passage that has always been a mainstay of my Christian walk, perhaps because it was one of the first Bible studies I was ever asked to lead. It forms the opening scene in that weird, wonderful, perplexing, stretching, glorious book, Revelation. John's vision of Christ walking in between his churches in Revelation 1 is vivid and unforgettable.

Life for Christian believers in the later years of the first century was turbulent and perilous. Hostility and even lethal threats could come from any corner: synagogues (infuriated by family members apparently rejecting their Judaism, as they saw it, and turning to Christ); local businesses (incensed by lost trade when this new religion challenged old loyalties, as in Philippi or Ephesus); the Roman state (determined to stamp out resistance or non-conformity and led by some deeply unpleasant and blood-thirsty leaders, of whom the most notorious were Nero and Domitian). It would be very odd if people were *not* intimidated or scared with all this going on. They needed all the reassurance they could get, confidence derived from realities that were truer than the horrors so many of them faced. That explains why the book of Revelation seems to be written as if all the TV dials had been turned up to eleven. Everything in the book seems more extreme. The colours really 'zing' and the audio levels are distorted and overpowering. But when someone is overwhelmed by persecution, this is perhaps the only way of getting an alternative perspective through to them.

The overarching point of Revelation, then, is to reassure and strengthen resolve. John regularly repeats the phrase 'the one who is victorious' – or as the 1984 NIV translation put it, 'he who overcomes' – in the hope that his book will be a key factor in their perseverance.[1] That is why John is granted a unique behind-the-scenes vision, a glimpse of the world as it appears from the heavenly throne room and not from a fetid Roman prison cell or on the run from an angry mob, or, as in John's case, while twiddling thumbs in exile on a minute Aegean island. There is suffering on earth – that is inescapable. Revelation gives hope that this suffering will never have the last word. The foundation for this is a vision of the risen Jesus himself.

Yet, it is this agenda that makes first encounters with the vision so disturbing as we shall discover.

A vision that drives us to despair

John hears a voice instructing him to write to seven churches in Roman Asia (from Ephesus to Laodicea). So naturally, he turns to see who is speaking.

> I turned round to see the voice that was speaking to me. And when I turned I saw seven golden lampstands, and among the lampstands was someone like a son of man, dressed in a robe reaching down to his feet and with a golden sash round his chest. The hair on his head was white like wool, as white as snow, and his eyes were like blazing fire. His feet were like bronze glowing in a furnace, and his voice was like the sound of rushing waters. In his right hand he held seven stars, and coming out of his mouth was a sharp, double-edged sword. His face was like the sun shining in all its brilliance.
> (Revelation 1:12–16)

These words may be very familiar. Yet even after reading them countless times, I still find them arresting. The writing is highly visual, cinematic even. But what would happen if a director tried to

---

1 Revelation 2:7, 2:11, 2:17, 2:26, 3:5, 3:12, 3:21, 15:2, 21:7. Sometimes rendered in other translations as 'the one who overcomes'.

capture John's multisensory experience on film? It would perhaps start comfortably enough in the fantasy genre. But here it rapidly slides into the realms of horror. Take the simple, clichéd technique for making a character other-worldly and intimidating by altering their eyes. What John sees when he looks round is clearly a person; he is described as 'someone like a son of man', a regular Old Testament idiom for human being. But he is so much more, even horrifyingly so. His eyes are 'like blazing fire'. It is unnerving to be addressed by someone with whom you cannot make eye contact. But then, this figure's entire face is hard to look at. It is like the shining sun (Revelation 1:16), and we all know the dangers of looking at that directly. This detail alone alerts us to the challenges in reading so-called apocalyptic writing. Press the visual details too far (as if attempting to paint them) and we will get confused. After all, if his face is like the sun, how is it possible to distinguish his eyes as blazing fires? That is to miss the point, of course. We are not meant to paint this book, but to interpret it. We need to seek the significance of the details in the grand scheme of the vision.

Everything about this figure's appearance is imposing and impressive. His full-length robe sets him apart, as if he were a senior Temple priest or royal prince. The golden sash is less common, however. Angels are the only others to wear them in John's book (Revelation 15:6). The white hair points to his ancient wisdom; feet like glowing bronze suggests a monumentality, as if he were a huge imperial statue come to life. But the focus of John's vision is not visual but aural. With John, we are overwhelmed by the noise. His 'voice was like the sound of rushing waters'. Stand beside a huge waterfall or on seaside rocks on a stormy day, you will know exactly what John is on about. It is impossible to hear or be heard. The water is too deafening. It might not be the most natural analogy to spring to mind for a compelling public speaker, say, or for a great Shakespearean actor seizing an audience's rapt attention with a monologue. But the point is clear. When this figure speaks, all other voices are eclipsed, drowned out by his majestic authority. To reinforce the point, John substitutes the imagery immediately, seeing a double-edged sword coming from the figure's mouth. That points back to Isaiah's servant describing how God made his 'mouth like a sharpened sword' (Isaiah 49:2).

Then in the New Testament, the author of Hebrews writes what might easily be taken as a commentary on this very Revelation passage, were it not for the fact that it was probably written earlier.[2] John almost certainly knew it.

> For the word of God is alive and active. Sharper than any double-edged sword, it penetrates even to dividing soul and spirit, joints and marrow; it judges the thoughts and attitudes of the heart. Nothing in all creation is hidden from God's sight. Everything is uncovered and laid bare before the eyes of him to whom we must give account.
> (Hebrews 4:12–13)

Notice that Hebrews also combines God's voice with his eyes here. That is precisely what one would expect, and it is a dynamic seen in all of the Old Testament's writing prophets. They hear from God, they view the world around them through God's eyes, and then they speak. God is living and active, he sees everything and always speaks truth and justice. Nothing is hidden. All of us 'must give account'. Like a sword in combat, God's words cut through the spin and smokescreens, exposing our dishonesty or pathetic excuses. None of these get us anywhere when standing before God. As Paul knew from personal experience, even privileged membership of God's old covenant people never made someone more righteous. 'Every mouth [will] be silenced and the whole world held account-able to God' (Romans 3:19).

If John's vision so far is not making you feel nervous or uneasy, then you have probably not been paying attention. The scene *is* intimidating. But then, why should an encounter with the living God be anything less? He created everything. He sustains everything. He owns everything. He sees everything. He knows

---

2 William Lane surveys several commentators' views and there is a consensus that the letter was written before the destruction of the Jerusalem Temple in AD 70. William L. Lane, *Hebrews 1–8*, vol. 47A, WBC (Dallas, TX: Word, 1991), p. lxvi.

everything. He rules everything. Just who do we think we are, presuming to amble into his throne room straight off the street? This is a God who inspires, and deserves, awe and reverence – and, by rights, deep terror. His holy purity has the white-hot intensity of a steel furnace – a concerning thought when recalling that nothing escapes his notice. The shock is that we are not used to speaking like this about Jesus. It's easy to see why God as presented in the Old Testament is feared and even dismissed because of such characteristics (albeit unjustly). But not Jesus. That just doesn't fit with his portrayal in the Gospels. But it does help to explain John's reaction to meeting Jesus, however: 'When I saw him, I fell at his feet as though dead' (Revelation 1:17).

This was as terrifying as it was overwhelming. But John will not have been surprised. There was biblical precedent for precisely the same thing. Isaiah reacted similarly to his vision of God's throne room (Isaiah 6:5). So did Peter after Jesus' miraculous fish trawl (Luke 5:8). If you are familiar at all with the Bible's accounts of divine encounters, this will come as no surprise. They inevitably provoke a sense of deep hopelessness and helplessness. With good reason. It is the response of God to that helplessness that should amaze us.

A vision that overwhelms us with wonder

At this point, John's fantasy-horror story appears to enter the realms of fairy tales. It seems too good to be true. This one 'like a son of man' shows a human side that nobody in the ancient world could ever have anticipated, let alone invented. He does what no classical god from Mount Olympus would dream of doing. 'Then he placed his right hand on me and said: "Do not be afraid"' (Revelation 1:17).

It is such a magnificently tender gesture. John lies prostrate on the floor. He does not describe his feelings, but he was most likely shaking in terror. Then, this majestic, cosmic figure presumably bends his knees to reach down to touch him. Perhaps it is just a hand on the shoulder, and then a gentle beckoning to look up, or even to stand. 'Do not be afraid!': the most common command in the Bible. We miss the significance of that if we zero in too quickly on its comfort since there *are* grounds for fear. God is nothing if not scary. The miracle is that he is also gentle. That is a rare combination indeed, certainly unique in the history of human religion. This cosmic Creator is full of such grace that he is unashamed to stoop to reassure a quivering creature.

It is only now that he identifies himself (as if we didn't know!): 'I am the First and the Last. I am the Living One; I was dead, and now look, I am alive for ever and ever! And I hold the keys of death and Hades' (Revelation 1:17–18).

Before this point, there have only been fleeting glimpses of Jesus as he really is. The most famous was his so-called Transfiguration. Right in front of Peter, James and John, Jesus transforms, his clothes becoming bleach-white and his appearance blinding (Mark 9:2–4). He is then joined by two old covenant great ones, Moses and Elijah. Their presence is significant for slightly differing reasons.

Moses had uniquely spent considerable time in the presence of Yahweh, so much so that he somehow reflected God's glory. Exodus describes how 'his face became radiant because he had spoken with the LORD', with the result that he had to be veiled for everybody else's protection (Exodus 34:29, 35). Moses, of course, was not permitted to enter the Promised Land, so there is something especially poignant and redemptive about this moment with Jesus. Moses at last makes an appearance within the borders of the land.

Elijah was the great prototype prophet after Moses and Samuel, called to speak truth to royal power. More importantly, he was granted the unique honour of a deathless end when he was whisked away during a whirlwind on a chariot of fire (2 Kings 2:11). During Jesus' lifetime, there were widespread hopes for Elijah to return as a prerequisite for the restoration of God's kingdom.

So here they both are: the one to whom the old covenant was first revealed, and the one who heralds the renewed kingdom.

Now in Revelation 1, John receives a far grander vision of what he merely glimpsed at the Transfiguration. The resurrection has now taken place. 'The Living One' who was dead is now 'alive for ever and ever'. The glory veiled during his earthly life was now on display. He is therefore 'the First and the Last'. This is the first of three occasions in the book where Jesus has this title and the last one fleshes it out: 'I am the Alpha and the Omega, the First and the Last, the Beginning and the End' (Revelation 22:13). The title is all-encompassing, one that claims precedence over the entire cosmos.

Jesus is the First

He is the First because he predates creation. He is the Lord of history and everything that is to come; the Lord of geography and every place of which we know nothing; the Lord of all, from the microscopic to the telescopic; the Lord of everything from the physical to the metaphysical. It all belongs to him, as both the one to create the cosmos and the one to redeem the cosmos. This has astonishing implications for our sense of reality. It means that whenever exploration or enquiry extends the boundaries of human knowledge, one thing is guaranteed. God in Christ is already there. He is there first because he created it first.

Jesus is the Last

He is the Last because he deserves the last word in any discussion on any topic. He is the ultimate purpose of everything that exists. It is for him and his glory, but this is no ego trip nor some kind of cosmic compliment-fishing expedition. Everything finds its fulfilment or restoration in him because that is the best thing that can possibly happen. It is good news because he is good. When we encounter even the very worst expressions of brokenness and pain, it means that there can be hope. Even when injustice seems to reign supreme, there will be justice. For those suffering wounds that never ease and diseases without cure, there will be healing. For even the most fractured and intractable divisions, there will be reconciliation. But it will never be a reconciliation that ignores the deep scars and grievances that caused those divisions. He is the Last because he knows what is needed in any and every circumstance. He is the Last because he will achieve what is needed in any and every circumstance.

This is the figure who lays a reassuring hand on John's shoulder and says, 'Do not be scared.' The one with the past and future sewn up is truly alive now in the present. What makes this particular title so striking is that it was previously reserved for Yahweh. In fact, it is only found in Isaiah, where it comes three times, and where it is designed to reinforce the uniqueness and exclusivity of God:

> This is what the LORD says – Israel's King and Redeemer, the LORD Almighty: I am the first and I am the last; apart from me there is no God.
> (Isaiah 44:6)

As in the New Testament, so with the book of Revelation: Jesus is identified with the God of Israel. Uniquely, exclusively, eternally.

A vision that assures us with hope

The living First and Last declares, 'I hold the keys of death and Hades' (Revelation 1:18). Now the fairy tale has shifted again and has become a manifesto, the announcement of an entirely new world. For as we have already seen, death is no longer to be feared. Possession of keys entails responsibility for whatever they unlock. But that is not all. They also represent authority. The resurrection demonstrates to the world that he has mastered death. The grave is no longer the end. Jesus is. He is truly the Last.

John had been present at nearly all the major moments of Jesus' earthly ministry. Only Peter seems to have witnessed more. John was there for the miracles, from the hidden to the spectacular. He heard so much of the teaching and perhaps was one of those keeping careful notes. He experienced the Transfiguration, the apparent catastrophe of the cross and the jaw-dropping wonder of the first Easter. He became a preacher of this story, something for which he was willing to pay any price, including exile to that puny, isolated rock Patmos (Revelation 1:9). He knew all too well about his own sinfulness and the threat this brought before the holiness of God.[3] He knew first-hand what it meant to be truly loved by his Lord.

Despite all this, even John seems to have needed this vision of the risen Christ. Within the span of just a few moments, he experiences despair at his sin, the gentleness of his Lord, and the wonder of a future beyond death. Jesus refuses to keep his resurrection to himself! It is available to all who come to him. Now that he has unlocked it, death is no longer a great barricade but a vast, open gate. In his grace, Jesus lifted him up as one who was acceptable to him, neither a helpless nor hopeless case. But that is not all. The vision anticipates what would eventually happen to John in real life and real death. He would be lifted up beyond the grave. Because he had Jesus.

A vision that reminds us of his presence

It is only now that John's vision broadens out from a deeply personal and intimate encounter. Having introduced himself, Jesus now gives him his marching orders. The vision was always intended for public consumption since it is to have global, even cosmic, importance.

> Write, therefore, what you have seen, what is now and what will take place later. The mystery of the seven stars that you saw in my right hand and of the seven golden lampstands is this: the seven stars are the angels of the seven churches, and the seven lampstands are the seven churches.
> (Revelation 1:19–20)

These seven lampstands are the first things John sees when he turns to identify the voice (1:12) because this figure was 'among' them. It now feels like an artist's installation designed to convey a spiritual truth visually. The issue, as with so much of the book of Revelation, is more to interpret what John is seeing than to try to visualise it (although, in this instance, it is a vivid scene). Each of

---

3 See, for example, John 16:4–11 and 1 John 1:8–10.

these lampstands, we are now told, is accompanied by a star, and Jesus is explicit about what that means. Each lampstand represents a church and its particular angel. Exactly why each church has an angel is unclear: we tend to assume each is a 'guardian angel' that people commonly refer to. It may well mean that. However, the word for angel simply means 'messenger', so it may perhaps simply refer to the pastor–teacher given by God to lead and guide the fellowship. Or perhaps each has a celestial overseer to lead the congregation's human elders. Or a combination. We cannot know for sure.

What is clear, however, is that Jesus stands among them, in authority and ownership. He is the one who was died and is now alive, the one to whom each and every church owes its existence. The one with blazing eyes that penetrate every darkness and every secret now walks through the lampstands. He sees and knows it

Figure 1 The seven churches of Revelation

all. It is no accident that there are seven churches here. As with Revelation's imagery, so with its numbers: we are not meant to calculate as much as we are to interpret. Seven is one of the most common biblical figures simply because of its creation precedent. It is therefore the symbolic number for completion, fulfilment, totality. When used of the churches in Asia Minor (now in modern Türkiye), the point is not their moral perfection – as we will see, these churches could hardly claim that – but the fact that they represent the entirety of God's Church, throughout the world and history. After all, there were plenty of other thriving churches in the region all the way along the coast and inland (some estimate between thirty and forty different congregations by AD 100, such as in Attalia, Colossae and Hierapolis).

The risen Christ weaves in between these representative congregations and what does he find? Many things to commend, several challenges to face, real dangers to confront. Some churches are doing better than others, inevitably, while one or two run the genuine risk of being closed down altogether (Ephesus and Sardis). In the next two chapters, each church receives Jesus' verdict in the form of a letter. They all follow the same stylised structure, flowing out of Jesus' identity as it is presented in John's opening vision but given resonance particular to each place. The letters are concise but dense, full of rich detail that rewards careful study. But for our purposes here, there is only space for an overview, showing how each letter echoes the other six (see Table 4). The key thing to recognise is that no church gets everything completely right, although Philadelphia comes close.[4]

The relevance of these ancient messages is clearer when taken together. We are meant to see the seven letters as a group. What Jesus writes to one is to be heeded by all, with these letters merely part of John's greater vision recorded for the benefit of all.

---

4 The persecution there seems particularly intense, warranting that alarming description of its source as the 'synagogue of Satan' in 3:9. Their story was not complete at the time of writing; they needed to persevere through the agonies of their persecution. But the risen Christ knew their suffering and sustained them within it.

Table 4 The seven churches in the book of Revelation

Seven churches	Ephesus 2:10–17	Smyrna 2:8–11	Pergamum 2:12–17	Thyatira 2:18–29	Sardis 3:1–6	Philadelphia 3:7–13	Laodicea 3:14–22
Jesus (see Revelation 1)	holds seven stars and walks among seven lampstands	is First and Last, who died and came to life again	has the sharp double-edged sword	has eyes like blazing fire and feet like burnished bronze	holds the seven spirits of God and seven stars	holy and true; holds key of David (what he opens can't be shut)	the Amen, faithful witness, ruler of God's creation
I know your deeds…	hard work and perseverance, intolerance of evil and falsehood; hatred of Nicolaitan practices	afflictions and poverty; slander of synagogue of Satan	where you live (Satan's throne); faithfulness (even to death – e.g. Antipas)	deeds, love and faith; service and perseverance; doing more than at first	reputation of life but actually dead; deeds unfinished in my sight	have kept word and not denied (Satan's synagogue will acknowledge); endured patiently	Lukewarm; not rich but pitiful, poor, blind, naked; I rebuke those I love
But I have this against you…	forsaken first love		teachers like Balaam – idolatry and sexual immorality; teachings of Nicolaitans	tolerate 'prophetess' Jezebel: sexual immorality and idols (she has had time to repent)			
Repent… Let him hear…	do what you did at first	don't fear suffering (prison, persecution ten days, death); be faithful	repent	hold on to the gospel not Jezebel	wake up: remember and obey what you heard; strengthen what's dying	hold on to your crown (I'm coming soon)	repent; buy gold, clothes and salve; open door and eat with Christ
If you do not repent	lampstand removed		I will fight with the sword of mouth	a bed of suffering (adulterers and children die); I search hearts and repay	I will come (like a thief in night)		
If you overcome (see Revelation 21–2)	right to eat from tree of life in paradise	not hurt by the second death	I will give hidden manna, white stone with new hidden name	I will give authority over nations (Psalm 2:9) and the morning star	a few who have not soiled their clothes – dressed in white and in book of life	a pillar in the temple – never leave; name of God, city and new name	right to sit with me on my throne (just as I did with Father)
Seven virtues	Love for Jesus	Enduring persecution	Teaching soundly	Intolerant of evil	Spiritually real	Patiently waiting	Humbly dependent

On the Lord's Day I was in the Spirit, and I heard behind me a loud voice like a trumpet, which said: 'Write on a scroll what you see and send it to the seven churches: to Ephesus, Smyrna, Pergamum, Thyatira, Sardis, Philadelphia and Laodicea.' (Revelation 1:10–11)

This explains why they have such resonance today. For nothing has altered Jesus' status since John's first-century exile on the island of Patmos. He is *still* the Lord, *still* the First and Last, *still* the possessor of the keys of death and Hades. He still wanders through the lampstands of his churches in Accra, Bogota and Chongqing, in Kolkata, Kuwait and Kyiv. He is Lord of each one; he loves each one; he strives for each one, bringing them to the maturity and perfection for which he died. So, we should fire up our imaginations again and think of him walking among the lampstands most familiar to us. What does he see? What must we learn? What must we change? How will we 'overcome'? Perhaps we should simply line up our own experience of our own discipleship and our own churches against the benchmark of the seven virtues that are the foundation of these letters.

Love Jesus

This might seem so obvious as to hardly need mentioning. Yet, the church in Ephesus had evidently gone wrong at this most basic level. They forgot their first love for Christ himself (Revelation 2:4). This must have been acutely painful for John especially since the city was his most likely home in old age. How could something this fundamental go awry? It is especially chilling that this took place in a church that valued sound teaching and ethical propriety so highly. The warnings for those seeking to maintain the moral high ground in an increasingly pagan and even hostile culture are stark indeed.

Teach what is sound

It would be all too easy to assume that the Ephesus mistake was to focus too much on so-called sound teaching, as if that explains why they lost sight of Jesus. But Jesus had no time for that way of thinking. He explicitly commends several churches for their good teaching in these letters. He saw no contradiction between good doctrinal understanding and loving devotion and worship. In fact, the latter is impossible without the former. Look carefully, and false teaching was the root of Pergamum's problems (2:14–15). Sound teaching is literally teaching that is healthy. That is why Paul, for example, is so concerned to commend it. In one of the last things he ever wrote, he advises Timothy to be committed to preaching the truth especially because there will always be people who 'will not put up with sound doctrine' (2 Timothy 4:3). In fact, earlier in the letter he describes the effect of Hymenaeus and Philetus, whose teaching spreads 'like gangrene' (2 Timothy 2:17).

Don't tolerate evil

It is one thing to teach the truth, it is another to uphold it. One of the problems in Thyatira, for example, was the way that an individual carried such sway that members were living in ways wildly inconsistent with the gospel. It seems their lifestyles hardly differed from those who wholeheartedly embraced the city's pagan culture of sexual immorality and idol-worship. So, the nickname Jesus gives this person is entirely apt since Jezebel was the Phoenician wife of Israel's King Ahab in the time of Elijah. She used her position to mandate the worship of Baal and Asherah as well as the brutal persecution of the prophets of Yahweh.

Tolerance is a virtue in the modern world, and that is something for which I am generally grateful. I would far rather live in a society that tolerates those who are different or unusual. The problem is when it is absolutised in such a way as to make discernment and distinctiveness difficult or even impossible. The problem in Thyatira was no *laissez-faire* attitude to members with quirks or oddities. It was a question of leadership, so that members were being drawn away from the Christian path and nobody seemed to do anything about it. This is akin to the person who knows that fog conceals a major accident on a motorway and watches as car after car hurtles towards disaster without trying to prevent it. That does not demonstrate a tolerant spirit, but a grotesque dereliction of compassion. For all their flaws, at least the Ephesians avoided that trap.

Keep it real

Human beings have always been good at presenting themselves well while concealing their true feelings and motives. A friend describes this as the difference between 'front-stage' and 'back-stage' reality. Detecting a discrepancy between the two was Jesus' charge against the Sardis church. 'I know your deeds; you have a reputation of being alive, but you are dead' (Revelation 3:1). We can become expert at giving the impression of spiritual life, identifying which phrases are most convincing, doing things that imply consistent behaviours without having to be consistent. This is, of course, the very definition of hypocrisy. We care more about the façade than the substance.

The great Scottish pastor and preacher, Robert Murray M'Cheyne once wrote: 'What a man is on his knees before God, that he is, and nothing more.'[5] It is perhaps a slight exaggeration, but not by much. He was driving at the perfect (and only) antidote to spiritual fraud: the cultivation of time spent in private with the Lord, to spend time in adoration for his grace, in confession of our sins, in petition for various needs (both for others and ourselves). Just as we as individual disciples need to cultivate this dependence on the risen Christ, so must our churches. We must be more concerned to be with him than to impress others (whether in other churches or in the culture around us). What matters is spiritual reality, not political and cultural influence, impressive performances or even crowds gathered in meetings with a real buzz. These might all feel alive; they can too easily conceal spiritual cancer backstage.

Endure persecution

There is an easily missed but stunning detail in Jesus' letter to the Smyrna church, although it perhaps does not seem so encouraging

---

5   D. A. Carson, *A Call to Spiritual Reformation* (Grand Rapids, MI: Baker, 1992), p. 16.

on first hearing. 'I tell you, the devil will put some of you in prison to test you, and you will suffer persecution for ten days' (Revelation 2:10). They were not the only church in the seven to be enduring the agony of public hatred and persecution: Pergamum and Philadelphia were in a similar boat. But Jesus knows what he is doing when he tells them their suffering is to be 'for ten days'. Whether we are to take that as a literal period, or, more likely, as a representative figure, the central point is that it is a known quantity. Their pain is not indefinite. Perhaps they felt like the Philadelphians who were conscious of their dwindling strength (Revelation 3:8). The crucial thing is that their suffering is not invisible. Their living Lord knows it all and, more significantly, had warned them. As John recorded in his Gospel, Jesus had made things very clear to the disciples:

> If the world hates you, keep in mind that it hated me first. If you belonged to the world, it would love you as its own. As it is, you do not belong to the world, but I have chosen you out of the world. That is why the world hates you.
> (John 15:18–19)

Most of us living in the West never come remotely close to the suffering that our brothers and sisters in the Middle East or in parts of Asia endure, so we must be wary of quickly resorting to words like persecution. Nevertheless, enduring something on the softer end of the spectrum is unpleasant enough – it might be mockery, or scorn, or an opponent's unwillingness to concede that we might have honourable motives, or deliberate spurning – the temptation can be to do whatever we can to minimise the shame regardless of the cost. We can easily justify this by a desire to preserve the good repute of the gospel, while, in reality, we are seeking a quieter life. No believer should ever seek out persecution (as if it were a perverse badge of honour or authenticity). Nor should we try to avoid it all costs. For church history proves again and again that it is often the mark of God's authentic church.

Wait patiently

Jesus' concern for all his followers – but especially for those in these seven churches – is that they overcome their trials. The rewards he holds out are an incentive in themselves: from eating the fruit from the tree of life to the right to sit with our risen Lord at God's right hand. But it will only come to those who are willing to be patient. We need to wait.

Patience is perhaps one Christian virtue that has become uniquely challenging in our technological and digitised age. Almost every single device regarded as essential in modern homes – so-called 'modern conveniences' – is designed to free us of the effort and time taken in the basic demands of life. Our ancestors would find our lives unrecognisable. I am not complaining, since I for one am very glad to avoid doing these tasks. The problem is that this seems to have contributed to a deep-seated restlessness and impatience in modern society. We cannot cope with waiting. As the strapline for a now defunct credit card used to say, 'It takes the waiting out of wanting.' The same seems true in our Christian lives. We want God's purposes – we just don't want to have to wait for them. Yet consider some of the Old Testament time frames. Abraham had to wait decades before the Lord's promise to make him the father of many nations was even remotely credible: he was one hundred years old when he became Isaac's father. Joseph languished in prison for thirteen years before his circumstances truly changed. Moses waited forty years before God used him to lead the people from Egypt.

The only way we will persevere as the saints of old did is if we remember that our risen Christ is with us. He walks among our lampstands. He sees our circumstances, which means he knows our pain. He walks with us in it all. What's more, we have his Spirit living within us. He makes it his special concern to develop what Paul identifies as the 'fruit of the Spirit', and at the heart of these is patience. By definition, it is not a virtue that can be developed quickly, but it is one that he longs for all of us. Encounter it in others and it is genuinely beautiful. To help us grow in it, we must imagine his presence with us as much as we decide to trust in him.

Depend humbly on God

Laodicea was one of Roman Asia's most successful and sophisticated cities. It was perhaps equivalent to one of those global
cities favoured by the jet-set and glamorous. It was a city to get
rich and be seen to be rich, a place to parade the latest fashions.
Unsurprisingly, its go-getting culture had a detrimental effect on
the Laodicean believers. They unwittingly aped the same culture
and harboured the same attitudes. This is what must have made
Jesus' rebuke so acutely painful.

> You say, 'I am rich; I have acquired wealth and do not need
> a thing.' But you do not realise that you are wretched, pitiful,
> poor, blind and naked. I counsel you to buy from me gold
> refined in the fire, so that you can become rich; and white
> clothes to wear, so that you can cover your shameful naked-
> ness; and salve to put on your eyes, so that you can see.
> (Revelation 3:17–18)

Appearances were deceptive. They thought they had it all, but in
spiritual terms they were in danger of ending up with nothing. But
that is the wonder of the gospel. God provides everything we truly
need, as opposed to what we assume or think we need. Just as the
prophet Isaiah promised eight centuries before him, this is true
wealth that costs us nothing but costs him everything. It is ours, for
free. 'Come, all you who are thirsty, come to the waters; and you
who have no money, come, buy and eat! Come, buy wine and milk
without money and without cost' (Isaiah 55:1).

The mark of a church that truly belongs to the risen Christ is
therefore that we grow to trust in his provision and kindness. We
trust him to provide for our needs. We trust him to go before us
while we trust that he walks among us. This is not pie-in-the-sky
wishful thinking, clutching irrationally at straws in the vague hope
that something might go right. Far from it. This is about following
our risen Lord through the earthy realities, challenges and confu-
sions of daily life. Even daily life in the modern world.

So as Jesus walks among the lampstands of your own church, what does he see?

Questions to consider

1 What is surprising about the way Jesus is presented in Revelation 1? How would this have helped the book's first readers?
2 What encouragements and challenges might Jesus have for your local church in the light of his seven letters (Revelation 2–3)?

9

Enduring life to eternal life: even better than perfection

There are many myths about doubt. The worst is that it automatically indicates spiritual failure, as if a true believer should never doubt anything. A complication arises because it is perfectly possible to use doubts as an excuse not to trust in God, whether consciously or not, but I suspect this is less common than some claim. For doubt is, in fact, essential to the process of establishing what we can believe, crucial for avoiding getting duped or deluded. But it is also simply a fact of life. We all have wobbles and stresses, triggered perhaps by changes in our circumstances, or health or relationships. Life is often bewildering and suffering is normal. Each change might present new challenges to long-held beliefs for the simple reason that we have never had to trust God in this situation before. Even great spiritual heroes have moments, or even extended periods, of doubt. Here Hudson Taylor, the pioneering missionary to China, describes the agony of losing several members of his family.

> A few months ago my home was full, now so silent and lonely
> – Samuel, Noel, my precious wife, with Jesus; the elder chil-
> dren far, far away, and even little T'ien-pao (Charles) in Yang
> Chow. Often, of late years, has duty called me from my loved
> ones, but I have returned, and so warm has been the welcome.
> Now I am alone. Can it be that there is no return from this
> journey, no home gathering to look forward to! Is it real, and
> not a sorrowful dream, that those dearest to me lie beneath
> the cold sod? Ah, it is indeed true.[1]

---

1   Marshall Broomhall, *Hudson Taylor: The man who believed God* (London: CIM, 1929), p. 161.

With remarkable candour, he expresses his deepest fears about the future and eternity. It is as if he must voice his doubt about the very truths that are foundational to his entire life and ministry. Only after voicing his doubts can he talk himself round and say, 'Ah, it is indeed true.' But do not underestimate his pain, even after this conviction was restored. His grief caused his own health to deteriorate significantly and he returned home to England to recover. He would remarry and live for another three decades but, if anything, the challenges and pains intensified. Nevertheless, just three months after that first passage, he could write this:

> No language can express what He has been and is to me. Never does He leave me; constantly does He cheer me with His love. …His own rest, His own peace, His own joy, He gives me. …Often I find myself wondering whether it is possible for her, who is taken, to have more joy in His presence than He has given me.[2]

What an astonishing shift. Sceptics may regard it as exaggerated or even absurd to go from putting on a stiff-upper lip to something verging on the ecstatic. His sense of God is palpable and real. He truly knows the living presence of the risen Christ with him. Who knows how many of us will also enjoy such depths of intimacy with God in this life? We are all different, as are our circumstances and challenges. What all believers do have in common, however, is the Lord. He is risen, alive, simultaneously enthroned in the courts of heaven and walking alongside each and every one of us. He accompanies us in the tensions that result from being a Christ follower in a broken world.

Enduring life: keep on keeping on

Paul nearly always began his letters in a format that was standard in the ancient world. Whereas we usually put the recipient at the start and the sender at the end, the old routine was to open with

---

2 Broomhall, *Hudson Taylor,* p. 161.

a personal introduction, immediately follow it with the recipient's name and address, and then perhaps include some sort of blessing or prayer before launching into the main body of the letter. Paul did make one innovation, however, and it was strange. See if you can spot it:

- 'To the church of God in Corinth, to those sanctified in Christ Jesus' (1 Corinthians 1:2).
- 'To God's holy people in Ephesus, the faithful in Christ Jesus' (Ephesians 1:1).
- 'To God's holy people in Colossae, the faithful brothers and sisters in Christ' (Colossians 1:2).
- 'To all God's holy people in Christ Jesus at Philippi' (Philippians 1:1).
- 'To the church of the Thessalonians in God the Father and the Lord Jesus Christ' (1 Thessalonians 1:1).

In each case, the recipients are given two locations, one earthly and one spiritual, just as we might share both our postal and email addresses. Of course, the spiritual address Paul describes is far from virtual, still less is it unreal. He describes a deeper, unbreakable reality, one that is entirely dependent on what God has done in uniting us to him. This means that at any given time, each believer and every fellowship genuinely exist in two places at once: the geographical and the theological. We might happen to live in Ephesus or Philippi, Edinburgh or Phnom Penh, but we are *simultaneously* in Christ.

Paul unpacks this idea in his Ephesian letter, and in doing so, reaches one of the great pinnacles of his writing, outlining the difference that the Jesus revolution has for a new believer.

But because of his great love for us, God, who is rich in mercy, made us alive with Christ even when we were dead in transgressions – it is by grace you have been saved. And God raised us up with Christ and seated us with him in the heavenly realms in Christ Jesus.
(Ephesians 2:4–6)

Notice how closely Paul ties the believer's experience with Christ's. He died, we were 'dead in transgressions'; he was restored to life, we were 'made alive with Christ'; he was raised up to heaven, we are 'raised up with Christ'; he is seated in the heavenly realms, we are 'seated with him' because we are 'in Christ Jesus'. Wherever Christ goes, we go. It's a truly bizarre thought. Inevitably, I have no clue where you are as you read this book, but I imagine that you are sitting down (hopefully on something comfortable). But you are highly unlikely to confuse your chosen reading spot for God's cosmic throne. Yet, Paul says that is precisely where we are *right now* if we are in Christ. We are in two places at once. We live on two planes of existence: the earthly and the heavenly.

That seems as absurd as it is impossible, but it is precisely what we need to imagine. Eternity with our Creator is where we truly belong, which is why this world will never ultimately satisfy. It explains the yearning we considered at the start of this book. If we are in Christ, reaching our final resting place is as inevitable as a boomerang returning to its thrower. Or perhaps a better analogy is the homing pigeon. Since long before even Old Testament times, people have recognised the remarkable capacity of these birds to navigate their way back to their nests from vast distances. More recently, research has shown that they can do so from over 1,000 miles (1,600 km) using an innate sense of the earth's magnetic field. We belong at home with Christ. While we are here in this world, this separation creates an inescapable tension. But in Christ, we will be home. This life is temporary, the life to come permanent; this creation is broken and damaged, the new creation restored and perfected; this world is full of sorrow and pain; the next a place of healing and comfort.

The tension between these two realities is what brings frustration and even pain, rather like doing the splits in gymnastics. In fact, this frustration is a good sign since it proves our anticipation of what God promises us. The more eager we are, the more frustrated we might feel. At one point, Paul uses the analogy of tents and buildings. He likens our finite and decaying bodies to tents in contrast to being 'clothed instead with our heavenly dwelling' (2 Corinthians 5:2).

> For while we are in this tent, we groan and are burdened, because we do not wish to be unclothed but to be clothed instead with our heavenly dwelling, so that what is mortal may be swallowed up by life.
> (2 Corinthians 5:4–5)

Who wouldn't want the perfect, eternal body?! With a prospect as astonishing and magnetic as heaven, why wouldn't we want to be there? But despite all his trials and hardships, Paul is emphatic about trusting God's timing for it. He is adamant that he will not speed up the process to get there even though 'to live is Christ and to die is gain'. This is because there is work for the kingdom to be done while he still can.

> Yet what shall I choose? I do not know! I am torn between the two: I desire to depart and be with Christ, which is better by far; but it is more necessary for you that I remain in the body. Convinced of this, I know that I will remain, and I will continue with all of you for your progress and joy in the faith.
> (Philippians 1:22–5)

He does not write out of a sense of his own indispensability. Rather he trusts in God's purposes, which means that for as long as he has the opportunities and capacity, he is content to keep on serving the gospel.

Later in the same letter, he reaffirms his convictions that God is the one to take the initiative and to sustain him in all he does. He is made right with God by God in Christ. It is all of grace. As we have seen repeatedly, only God could give us new life. But does this mean we are passive before the life to come, as if the only thing we can do is to wait patiently on a station platform for the train to arrive. By no means! Reflecting on the resurrection of all those who have already died in Christ, Paul writes:

> Not that I have already obtained all this, or have already arrived at my goal, but I press on to take hold of that for which

Christ Jesus took hold of me. Brothers and sisters, I do not consider myself yet to have taken hold of it. But one thing I do: forgetting what is behind and straining towards what is ahead, I press on towards the goal to win the prize for which God has called me heavenwards in Christ Jesus.
(Philippians 3:12–14)

Notice how active Paul is: he presses on; he strains towards what is ahead; he presses on. Picture the sweat and exertion of marathon runners giving everything they have got to cross the finishing line. They are focused, determined, relentless. They have a one-track mind and, despite the hours and distance required, they never waver. Like them we have the joy at the finishing line, in our case when we meet our Christ and Lord face to face. But there is one essential difference between long-distance athletes and persevering Christians. The athletes must rely on their own resources whereas we have Christ. He is indispensable, giving us everything we need to get there in the first place. We 'take hold' of the goal because he first 'took hold of' us. We 'press on towards the goal' because God called us 'heavenwards in Christ Jesus' for that prize. That is our confidence.

Our efforts are *only* in response to a divine call.

Our perseverance *wholly* depends on a divine initiative.

Our eternal future rests *entirely* on a divine grace.

The Spirit with his Church therefore cries out the good news. 'Come! Let the one who is thirsty come; and let the one who wishes take the free gift of the water of life' (Revelation 22:17). In response, we cry out to the one who promises that he is coming soon, 'Amen. Come, Lord Jesus' (Revelation 22:20).

Even better than perfection

Over decades, the entrepreneur Richard Branson has forged a quirky but lucrative path, building on the unprecedented success of his new Virgin label's gamble on Mike Oldfield's 1973 album, *Tubular Bells*. He has diversified into retail, telecommunications, banking, airlines, train companies and most recently, space tourism. The Virgin group has had its financial ups and downs over the years, but Branson remained at its centre until retiring as chairman in 2009. He now spends much of his time on his private island in the British Virgin Islands, Necker Island. It was completely uninhabited in 1979 when he bought it for only £120,000. He has since invested over £10 million to turn it into a luxury resort accommodating over fifty guests, as well as his own residence. It has everything you could possibly want in an exclusive hotel: panoramic views of a turquoise sea from Balinese-style thatched villas, infinity pools and pristine beaches, gourmet food and vintage wines, spa treatments, tennis and water sports, marine transport to a nearby airport all included. It is many people's idea of paradise. Leafing through the brochure, I found myself agreeing and felt pangs of longing. The catch is the price: between US$5,000 and $8,000 per couple per night, for a minimum of four nights. If you prefer, why not make considerable savings by block-booking the entire resort, for a mere $135,000 per night? Despite hoping that I would be more virtuous in the stewardship of my funds if I was a millionaire, I can quite see how I might find ways to justify the expense! After all, where else can you enjoy a private paradise while hobnobbing with A-listers and presidents?

I have found myself daydreaming about the place from time to time, ever since first watching an advert for Necker years ago.[3] It is a beautifully paced film, plotted as a wander through the island inspecting all the delights on offer. It is only when you get to its punchline, you realise something strange about it. The voiceover concludes, 'The only thing missing... is you!' You suddenly realise that throughout, no guests are seen anywhere, only staff putting final touches to their preparations. So, you find yourself thinking, 'Yes, that's exactly where I want to be! In fact, that's where I need to be!' It is paradise, a dream, a utopia.

Or is it?

---

3   Necker Island, bestdestination, YouTube, 2009, https://www.youtube.com/watch?v=et54ONvmNsI, (accessed 18 January 2024).

The origins of the word *utopia* are fascinating. Sir Thomas More invented it in 1516 as an ingenious pun. He derived it from the Greek word *topos* meaning 'a place' (the word topology is derived from it). But then onto the front, he added another Greek word *eu* meaning 'good' (from which eulogy comes). 'Eutopia' is therefore a good place, a place of perfection, or even heaven. The pun works because in Greek, the word *eu* sounds almost identical to *ou*, the word for 'no' or 'not'. So, when he creates his new word, More deliberately makes it ambiguous, by missing out the first letter. The point is simple. Does a truly good place exist? Or is it no place, an impossible place, a hollow fantasy? The only thing missing is... what exactly? What would make it real? What would make it possible?

Necker Island is spectacular. But it can never offer a total escape from the realities of the world. The region is notorious for its hurricane seasons and only a few years ago one of the island's main buildings burnt to the ground. Then what of the people who visit? No doubt most have an unforgettable stay, but it is not hard to imagine competing egos, guests' incompatible demands and the challenges we all face when living cheek by jowl with others, even for a short time. Stir in the entitlement and insecurities that too often characterise the super-wealthy and things are bound to get... complicated. No one can fail to bring their own baggage into any environment: hurts and scars, fears and insecurities, sins and selfishness. This is ultimately what cripples every human attempt to create a paradise. For as history has taught us, every attempt to build heaven on earth will result in hell. The only thing missing is you? Me? Seriously?

God's dwelling-place

There is a simple reason why human attempts at creating paradise are doomed to failure: the human heart. That is a conundrum only God can solve. This is what makes John's glimpse of heaven at the end of Revelation so stirring. For what is the one feature missing from every human attempt at heaven? It has been staring us in the face from the opening pages of Scripture: our Creator. At its epicentre, the Bible's celestial vision has the one person who makes it even possible. The miracle is that he makes it available to those who, left to their own devices, would devastate it.

> I saw the Holy City, the new Jerusalem, coming down out of heaven from God, prepared as a bride beautifully dressed for her husband. And I heard a loud voice from the throne saying, 'Look! God's dwelling-place is now among the people, and he will dwell with them. They will be his people, and God himself will be with them and be their God.'
> (Revelation 21:2–3)

God wants to dwell with his people so he will make it happen. That is the ultimate victory of Christ. All that is implied by the simple description of the Church, 'prepared as a bride, beautifully dressed for her husband'. There will be sharp intakes of breath and gasps when she appears, as in human weddings, because nobody could previously have believed quite how beautiful she could be. But on the day, she is stunning. Christ her husband has made her beautiful. There will be no blot or blemish, no disfigurement or scars; just healing, restoration, new creation.

What is true for the Church is true for the cosmos.

> 'He will wipe every tear from their eyes. There will be no more death' or mourning or crying or pain, for the old order of things has passed away.
> (Revelation 21:4, quoting Isaiah 25:8)

That list is startling for what is missing. Sadness, suffering and sickness are all absent. They are banished forever because death is banished from God's presence.

God's throne-city

Some get nervous at this point. Something lasting forever is both inconceivable and intimidating. We might complain about a journey or a speech for lasting an eternity. In other words, it seems the definition of extended boredom. For in life, don't we all know that even the best things pale? Nothing lasts forever. Everything in this life decays or breaks eventually. Even the most thrilling roller-coaster ride is dull on the thirty-seventh round. That is certainly the conclusion reached by several characters in the hit TV comedy about eternity, *The Good Place*. Yet, as Peter reminds us, the inheritance we have in store, will never 'perish, spoil or fade' (1 Peter 1:4). The mistake is not comparing like with like. This means this future hope is, by definition, of a different order. As ever, C. S. Lewis is helpful here about 'the facetious people' who scorn an 'eternity playing harps'.

> if they cannot understand books written for grown-ups, they should not talk about them. All the scriptural imagery (harps, crowns, gold, etc.) is, of course, a merely symbolical attempt to express the inexpressible. Musical instruments are mentioned because for many people (not all) music is the thing known in the present life which most strongly suggests ecstasy and infinity. …People who take these symbols literally might as well think that when Christ told us to be like doves, He meant that we were to lay eggs.[4]

The most inconceivable aspect of heaven is the very thing that provokes this ecstasy: being in the presence of God. Yet that will preoccupy us with more grounds for wonder than could fill an eternity. John can only pass on to us the minutest glimpse of his vision, which is itself an infinitesimally small speck from the full breadth of the experience of living it. But with Lewis's insights about biblical imagery in mind, be amazed afresh by John's second glance at God's throne room.

> Then the angel showed me the river of the water of life, as clear as crystal, flowing from the throne of God and of the Lamb down the middle of the great street of the city. On each side of the river stood the tree of life, bearing twelve crops of

---

4   C. S. Lewis, *Mere Christianity*, 26th ed. (London: Collins, 1990), p. 119.

fruit, yielding its fruit every month. And the leaves of the tree are for the healing of the nations. No longer will there be any curse. The throne of God and of the Lamb will be in the city, and his servants will serve him. They will see his face, and his name will be on their foreheads. There will be no more night. They will not need the light of a lamp or the light of the sun, for the Lord God will give them light. And they will reign for ever and ever.

(Revelation 22:1–5)

This draws threads together from as far back as Genesis as well as others scattered throughout Scripture. Just as the Bible provides two different but compatible angles on creation (in Genesis 1–2), so Revelation seems to offer a parallel, with two, slightly different takes on the new creation in God's heaven (in Revelation 21–2). If Genesis 1 shows off God's grand scheme while Genesis 2 homes in on the man and woman in the garden, Revelation 21 shows us the new Jerusalem while Revelation 22 highlights the restoration of all that was lost from Eden.

The Bible's original vision of paradise was entirely organic and rural, a beautiful garden home. It provides every source of sustenance and beauty human beings could possibly need, not merely to survive but to thrive. It was perfection. But we were banished from the garden to prevent our access to the tree of life. Sin's curse has loomed large over every single life born 'east of Eden'. When those people gathered together, disaster ensued, which is why cities have such negative connotations in the Bible. The archetype was Babylon, where humanity gathered together to take on God by building a colossal 'tower that reaches to the heavens' (Genesis 11:4). The assumption is that the larger the crowd, the greater the sin. It is more than unexpected, therefore, to find that John's heavenly vision places a city at its heart. The crucial ingredients from Eden are present, but somehow they have been merged with a glistening, jewel-encrusted city. This is no rural, escapist idyll that might be used as the backdrop for Bible verse posters. It is a bustling and thriving urban environment. That is emphatically not what many expect to be a central feature of heaven. Odder still, as we see in Revelation 21, this city has come *down* to us. People commonly speak of 'going to heaven when we die' when in fact the Bible insists that heaven has come to earth. Just as with Jesus' resurrection body, God's heaven is a very earthy, material reality.

The tree of life is there, but weirdly straddles the city's grand boulevard, which also contains the river of life flowing from the throne. It is fantastical but wonderful. For God has redeemed even cities because he has eradicated sin's curse. Now the countless peoples of the world gather without the slightest fear or anxiety it will collapse or degenerate. The tree of life does not simply give access to eternal life but also healing for all that was sick. As John saw in his original encounter, Jesus is as bright and awesome as the sun. But we will see his face, we will be identified as his. This means there will never be darkness. He is the light of the world. We will be united to him in every conceivable way. There will no longer be a gap between the now and not yet. All will be an *eternal* now. All because Jesus has conquered death once and for all. Because of Jesus there is truly life after life. This is a garden-city fit for kings and queens. Hard though it is to get our minds round this, if the Garden of Eden was perfection, the Garden-City of Jerusalem is even better than perfection.

This means there is one simple litmus test for every dream, every ambition, every grand ideology, every world-shaping agenda, every philosophy, every religion: *who sits at its centre*? If it is not the uniquely risen Lord Jesus Christ, then whatever its merits (which may be considerable), it has no ultimate or eternal power. Only he has found the means to heal the nations and cure creation's brokenness. Only he has reversed sin's curse. Only he has been victorious over death. There is no one else. So, it is hard to improve on the words of John Dyer, the eighteenth-century Welsh poet and pastor, when he said, 'A man may go to heaven without health, without riches, without honours, without learning, without friends; but he can never go there without Christ.'

I close with a prayer that John Stott wrote and used to pray at the start of every day. It has a striking mix of intimate, affectionate friendship and awe-filled wonder and dependence. I can think of no better way of drawing all the threads of this book together while we live in anticipation of our life after life.

> Good morning, Heavenly Father,
> good morning, Lord Jesus,
> good morning, Holy Spirit.
>
> Heavenly Father, I worship you as the creator and sustainer of the universe.
> Lord Jesus, I worship you, Saviour and Lord of the world.
> Holy Spirit, I worship you, sanctifier of the people of God.
> Glory to the Father, and to the Son, and to the Holy Spirit.
>
> Heavenly Father, I pray that I may live this day in your presence and please you more and more.
> Lord Jesus, I pray that this day I may take up my cross and follow you.
> Holy Spirit, I pray that this day you will fill me with yourself and cause your fruit to ripen in my life: love, joy, peace, patience, kindness, goodness, faithfulness, gentleness, and self-control.
>
> Holy, blessed, and glorious Trinity, three persons in one God, have mercy upon me.
>
> Amen.[5]

Questions to consider

1 How would you respond to someone who was convinced that heaven sounded really boring?
2 How does the prospect of eternity with Christ influence your plans and ambitions? How can we help one another to have greater confidence in its reality?

---

5 John Stott, *Pages from a Preacher's Notebook*, ed. Mark Meynell (Bellingham, WA: Lexham, 2020), p. 280.

Appendix

Evidence for Jesus' resurrection: some very brief pointers

It matters that Jesus actually did rise from the dead in space and history. For if he did not, then we can dismiss everything that this book has been exploring; our faith is useless and 'we are of all people most to be pitied', as Paul put it (1 Corinthians 15:19). Here, then, is the briefest summary of the key aspects of the historical evidence, with some suggested further reading for those who want to go deeper.

What God is like

- What sort of God could not overcome death? If he could not, would he be worthy of our worship and adoration?
- Why wouldn't God overcome death? If God did make everything in the universe, why would he be only concerned for the spiritual realms and not the material? Genesis 1 shows very clearly that he declared the material realm to be good. So, if he did overcome death and achieve a resurrection of some sort, why would it be anything less than physical?

What the New Testament writers announce

- There is no evidence that the New Testament writers regarded Jesus' resurrection as anything less than physical (despite the claims of some modern scholars). They did not see it as a metaphor or symbol. After all, that would have been far easier to proclaim in a Greek-influenced culture which saw the material world as inherently inferior if not evil. Paul would have encountered far less hostility or incomprehension had he simply said that Jesus was *spiritually* alive. Instead, he preached that Jesus was raised from the dead (1 Corinthians 15:15).

- The Gospel writers pointed to his risen physicality. He is clearly no apparition.
  - 'Suddenly Jesus met them. "Greetings," he said. They came to him, clasped his feet and worshipped him' (Matthew 28:9).
  - 'When he was at the table with them, he took bread, gave thanks, broke it and began to give it to them' (Luke 24:30).
  - 'Then he said to Thomas, "Put your finger here; see my hands. Reach out your hand and put it into my side. Stop doubting and believe"' (John 20:27).
- If we work through the apostles' sermons recorded by Luke in the book of Acts, it is striking how central the proclamation of the resurrection was. At the very start, Peter says at Pentecost, 'God has raised this Jesus to life, and we are all witnesses of it' (Acts 2:32).

The dead don't rise, do they?

This seems a perfectly reasonable assumption because none of us have met anyone who has actually been raised from the dead.

- Note that we are discussing *resurrection* rather than *resuscitation* here. Through advances in medical science and technology, there are stories of people coming 'back to life' after being pronounced dead. They have been resuscitated. But each and every one of them will still die. Resurrection means never having to face death again.
- Of course, based on historical precedent, resurrection is *highly unlikely*; from a statistical perspective it is impossible! But strictly speaking, if dealing with a God active in the world he created, it must at least be theoretically possible. We should not prejudge the question.

But perhaps Jesus didn't actually die on the cross?

This is a classic rebuttal used by various sceptics.

- Crucifixion was horrific – so terrible, in fact, that Roman law considered the punishment too barbaric for criminals with the status of Roman citizens – but it was relatively common. For example, when Spartacus led the slave revolt in 70 BC, hundreds of captured slaves were crucified along the Appian Way (one of the main arteries into Rome). Victims tended to die slowly, often of asphyxiation when they finally lost the strength to lift the torso high enough to breathe. Bones were dislocated and broken; their body's weight hung from the nails that fixed them to the wood. Whatever the final cause of death, intolerable agony was guaranteed. Even if they were rescued after a time, victims would be crippled for whatever remained of their lives.

- Roman and Jewish sources tell us a great deal about the system. One Jewish writer, Josephus, even mentions the fact that Jesus was crucified. There are some difficulties with the text since it is likely to have been embellished by Christian copyists in subsequent centuries (with additions about Jesus' resurrection). But many scholars accept that the core lines about his crucifixion were original. It was widely believed Jesus did die.[1]

- John 19:34–5 reads like an eye-witness account. Why else include this detail unless it stood out as odd or notable? 'One of the soldiers pierced Jesus' side with a spear, bringing a sudden flow of blood and water. The man who saw it has given testimony, and his testimony is true.' He could never have appreciated the medical significance of this detail, but we now know that around ninety minutes after death, the blood separates into plasma (a red sludge) and serum (clear like water).

- Could Jesus have swooned and then convinced the world that not only was he alive and well but in fact had never felt better in his life? How would he have concealed the fact that nearly all his bones were damaged or dislocated, then after not eating or drinking for a couple of days, manage to dislodge a huge

---

1   R. T. France, *Jesus the Radical* (Leicester: IVP, 1989), p. 30.

boulder, sneak past a cohort of Roman soldiers and then walk seven miles towards Emmaus (see Matthew 27:60, 66 and Luke 24:13). That would take a miracle.

Was Jesus' tomb actually empty?

Did the women go to the wrong tomb that first morning? Did Peter and John then make the same mistake? This makes no sense, for several reasons.

- The Gospels note how Jesus was buried in a tomb belonging to a wealthy family, that of Joseph of Arimathea. This was no paupers' mass grave. As such, it was easy to identify. The one thing that the authorities feared was rumours circulating about Jesus rising (not that anyone really believed he would) (Matthew 28:11–15). So, establishing they had the correct burial plot would the *first* thing to check. But the disciples would have wanted to be sure of that as well. Three of the four Gospel accounts make a point of noting that the women all 'saw the tomb' and so could identify its location (Matthew 27:61; Mark 15:47; Luke 23:55).
- The authorities were paranoid that people might steal Jesus' body in order to substantiate the rumours. Why else guard the tomb of a penniless, migrant preacher? But who would steal it?
  - The Jewish or Roman authorities? What possible motive would they have? And they would have simply needed to produce the body to crush the rumours.
  - Grave robbers? Why steal from the only guarded tomb in Jerusalem? What was there to steal? Why on earth would they take the body but not the burial cloths?
  - The disciples themselves? What possible motive would they have? As we have seen repeatedly, the disciples found the likelihood of Jesus rising impossible to get their heads around. They really didn't expect it to happen in reality. The two on the Emmaus Road spoke for many no doubt when they left Jerusalem thinking it was all over, even after the rumour that he had risen started spreading (Luke 24:21).

But suppose just one of the disciples did and fooled the others? Quite apart from the challenge of fooling the guards, it is a stretch to imagine that he did this to perpetuate what he knew was a complete lie, especially when all but one of the Twelve (John himself) ended up being martyred for preaching the risen Christ. People do die for delusions but only when they believe they are true. Nobody dies for a lie.

- It is no small fact that it was women who found the tomb empty that first Easter morning. Not only did it show them special honour as loyal friends of Jesus, but it was a detail no ancient writer would invent. Shocking though it is to modern sensibilities, women were not regarded as reliable witnesses in a Roman or Jewish court.
- Joseph of Arimathea's tomb never became a place of veneration or pilgrimage in the first or second centuries AD. We know from Peter's speech at Pentecost that King David's tomb was identifiable in Jerusalem (Acts 2:29). If Jesus had stayed dead, isn't it likely that at least some admirers would have memorialised him in some way (however great their disappointment might have been)?

Did people actually meet Jesus?

Matthew, Luke and John each describe encounters with the risen Jesus.[2] But the most striking account comes from Paul. He mentions that various disciples met Jesus after that first Sunday on different occasions. He then notes that 'he appeared to more than five hundred of the brothers and sisters at the same time, most of whom are still living, though some have fallen asleep' (1 Corinthians 15:6).

- Did Paul invent these appearances? 1 Corinthians is one of the two earliest documents of the New Testament, dated to less than twenty years after the events in question. This makes it almost unique when placed alongside the entire corpus of

---

2 To read expositions of these particular chapters, see Mark Meynell, *The Resurrection: First encounters*, revised ed. (Leyland: 10Publishing, 2013).

ancient documents in our possession. He is adamant that what he preaches is something that was passed down to him. Others knew it before him (1 Corinthians 15:3). Furthermore, the implication of most of the five hundred still being alive is that it was still possible to talk to them!

- Perhaps these are hallucinations? Impossible. Hallucinations are profoundly personal and usually derived from an individual's deepest fears or longings. They are products of significant mental distress or illness. It would itself be miraculous for even a handful to experience the same thing. Furthermore, they tend to occur over long periods with regularity. The resurrection appearances happen in a confined period of time, in different ways and to varying numbers.

How else do you explain the existence of the Church?

After Jesus was executed, the disciples were terrified. They knew what was at stake. Why else would their ringleader, Peter, be too scared even to admit having met Jesus on the day he was arrested? *Something* must have happened to transform him and the others into men and women willing to stake everything on Jesus being alive.

- If Jesus was not alive, why would the disciples preach that he was, on pain of death?
- If Jesus was not alive, what explanation could there be for the existence of the Church?
- If Jesus was not alive, what explanation could there be for the seismic sociological change of shifting the day of the week set aside for worship from Saturday to Sunday? All the first believers were Jewish and marking the Sabbath was core to their religious identity and heritage (going back centuries). Moving the meeting day was arbitrary and uncalled for without good reason.

The accumulative weight of evidence points to one simple fact: *Jesus rose from the dead.*

Further reading

Frank Morrison, *Who Moved The Stone?* (Authentic, 2006)
A classic, first published in 1930, by a journalist who set out to disprove the resurrection.

Rebecca McLaughlin, *Is Easter Unbelievable?* (Good Book Company, 2023)
Up to date, brief and readable.

John Dickson, *Is Jesus History?* (Good Book Company, 2019)
Accessible overview of the historicity of Jesus by a scholar of the classical world.

Michael Licona, *The Resurrection of Jesus* (Apollos, 2010)
This is a doorstop (at 643 pages) but if you want to go deep, this is the place to go!

Keswick Ministries

Our purpose

Keswick Ministries exists to inspire and equip Christians to love and live for Christ in his world.

God's purpose is to bring his blessing to all the nations of the world (Genesis 12:3). That promise of blessing, which touches every aspect of human life, is ultimately fulfilled through the life, death, resurrection, ascension and future return of Christ. All of the people of God are called to participate in his missionary purposes, wherever he may place them. The central vision of Keswick Ministries is to see the people of God equipped, inspired and refreshed to fulfil that calling, directed and guided by God's Word in the power of his Spirit, for the glory of his Son.

Our priorities

There are three fundamental priorities which shape all that we do as we look to serve the local church.

Hearing God's Word: the Scriptures are the foundation for the church's life, growth and mission, and Keswick Ministries is committed to preach and teach God's Word in a way that is faithful to Scripture and relevant to Christians of all ages and backgrounds.

Becoming like God's Son: from its earliest days, the Keswick movement has encouraged Christians to live godly lives in the power of the Spirit, to grow in Christlikeness and to live under his lordship in every area of life. This is God's will for his people in every culture and generation.

Serving God's mission: the authentic response to God's Word is obedience to his mission, and the inevitable result of

Christlikeness is sacrificial service. Keswick Ministries seeks to encourage committed discipleship in family life, work and society, and energetic engagement in the cause of world mission.

Our ministry

Keswick Convention. The Convention attracts some 12,000 to 15,000 Christians from the UK and around the world to Keswick every summer. It provides Bible teaching for all ages, vibrant worship, a sense of unity across generations and denominations, and an inspirational call to serve Christ in the world. It caters for children of all ages and has a strong youth and young adult programme. And it all takes place in the beautiful Lake District – a perfect setting for rest, recreation and refreshment.

Keswick fellowship. For more than 140 years, the work of Keswick has had an impact on churches worldwide, not just through individuals being changed but also through Bible conventions that originate or draw their inspiration from the Keswick Convention. Today, there is a network of events that shares Keswick Ministries' priorities across the UK and in many parts of Europe, Asia, North America, Australia, Africa and the Caribbean. Keswick Ministries is committed to strengthening the network in the UK and beyond, through prayer, news and cooperative activity.

Keswick teaching and training. Keswick Ministries is developing a range of inspiring, equipping, Bible-centred teaching and training that focuses on 'whole-of-life' discipleship. This builds on the same concern that started the Convention: that all Christians live godly lives in the power of the Spirit in all spheres of life in God's world. Some of the events focus on equipping. They are smaller and more intensive. Others focus on inspiring. Some are for pastors, others for those in other forms of church leadership, while many are for any Christian. All courses aim to see participants return home refreshed to serve.

Keswick resources. Keswick Ministries produces a range of books, devotionals and study guides as well as digital resources to inspire and equip Christians to live for Christ. The printed resources focus on the core foundations of Christian life and mission and help Christians in their walk with Christ. The digital resources make teaching and sung worship from the Keswick Convention available in a variety of ways.

Our unity

The Keswick movement worldwide has adopted a key Pauline statement to describe its gospel inclusivity: 'all one in Christ Jesus' (Galatians 3:28). Keswick Ministries works with evangelicals from a wide variety of church backgrounds, on the understanding that they share a commitment to the essential truths of the Christian faith as set out in our statement of belief.

Our contact details

T: 01768 780075
E: info@keswickministries.org
W: www.keswickministries.org
Mail: Keswick Ministries, Rawnsley Centre, Main Street, Keswick, Cumbria, CA12 5NP, England